OPERA
LOVER'S COOKBOOK

OPERA
LOVER'S COOKBOOK
Menus for Elegant Entertaining

FRANCINE SEGAN

Foreword by RENÉE FLEMING   Photographs by MARK THOMAS

STEWART, TABORI & CHANG · NEW YORK

DEDICATION

This book is dedicated to Max Segan, who is always willing to help on my cookbook projects, especially when it's time to eat!

Published in 2006 by Stewart, Tabori & Chang
An imprint of Harry N. Abrams, Inc.

Text copyright © 2006 Francine Segan
Food photographs copyright © 2006 Mark Thomas
Additional credits appear on page 212

Library of Congress Cataloging-in-Publication Data:
Segan, Francine.
  Opera lover's cookbook : menus for elegant entertaining / by Francine Segan ; foreword by Renée Fleming ; photographs by Mark Thomas in association with The Metropolitan Opera Guild.
     p. cm.
  Includes index.
  ISBN-13: 978-1-58479-536-0
  ISBN-10: 1-58479-536-0
  1. Entertaining. 2. Cookery, International. 3. Menus. 4. Opera. I. Title.

TX731.S437 2006
642'.4—dc22
                              2006013432

Designers: Galen Smith and LeAnna Weller Smith
Photo Researcher: Joseph B. Oerke
Production Manager: Jane Searle

The text of this book was composed in Eplica Book, Bickham Script, and Gotham.

Opposite: Luciano Pavarotti in *L'Elisir d'Amore*
Preceding pages: *La Traviata*
Following page: *Turandot*

Printed and bound in China
10 9 8 7 6 5 4 3 2 1

HNA
harry n. abrams, inc.
a subsidiary of La Martinière Groupe

115 West 18th Street
New York, NY 10011
www.hnabooks.com

CONTENTS

Acknowledgments

Deepest gratitude goes to the Metropolitan Opera Guild and David Dik, Managing Director, for allowing me to share in this delightful project. I am indebted to Arlene Bender, Director of Merchandising, who conceived of the book and suggested the *Hansel and Gretel* children's party. Special thanks to Joseph Oerke—audio, video, and book buyer for the Met Guild—who was a constant source of guidance, advice, and support. Joseph is one of the most effective and efficient professionals it has ever been my honor to work with.

Heartfelt appreciation to F. Paul Driscoll, editor-in-chief of *Opera News*, for his sage advice, especially on the Gilbert & Sullivan chapter. F. Paul made a profound impact on this work, including naming many of the chapters. Thanks to Oussama Zahr, researcher extraordinaire, for his meticulous fact-checking, and for scouring librettos and source materials to suggest and supplement sidebars. His knowledge and appreciation of opera is evidenced in each and every chapter.

Special appreciation to photographer Mark Thomas for the book's gorgeous photographs and to Nancy Thomas, prop stylist, for her artistic eye. Thanks to William Smith, food stylist, for all his tasteful work.

Gratitude to S. J. Shrubsole Antiques and James McConnaughy for the loan of the fine antique nutmeg graters, photographed in the bel canto chapter, and the nut picks in the French chapter.

Huge thanks to Marc Levy, opera aficionado, for guidance throughout. Marc provided invaluable suggestions on recipes and sidebars in much of the book, especially the Gilbert & Sullivan, verismo, and tapas chapters.

Gratitude to Lee Elman for all his learned advice, particularly on the German-language chapter. His love of opera is infectious!

Many thanks to John Forster—my favorite musician and performer—for all his help, most especially for the idea of the bel canto and verismo chapters and for naming Osso *Nabucco*! Thanks to the Vassilaros family.

Special thanks to Brian Shields for recipe input and all his help on the *Hansel and Gretel* chapter.

Gratitude goes to Seth Rogovoy, Sandra Ourusof, Sally and Mike Roth, and Victor Bond—composer and conductor—for their valued assistance and counsel.

Special appreciation to John Patrick Shanley, admirer of all things Italian, for his help with the Puccini chapter.

Every recipe in this cookbook has been tested and retested to ensure that the results achieved in my kitchen will occur in yours. I am deeply indebted to the gourmet home cooks who served as recipe testers.

Thanks to Karen Broido of Davis, California, whose love of opera all began thanks to her wonderful husband, Irv, her favorite recipe tester. Thanks to Kathy Hunt—writer and wonder in the kitchen—and to J. C. S. Deering, Rosalie Pavone, Kathryn McGowan, Amber Normandin, and Lori Shields for excellent recipe testing.

A standing ovation to Joanna Barouch—recipe tester, opera buff, musician, truffle hunter, and macaroon maker—for all her advice on recipes, lyrics, and sidebars.

My love and appreciation to my husband, Marc Segan—inventor, theater producer, and recipe taster—for all his love, devotion, and wisdom, and to my children, Samantha and Max, for the joy they bring me.

My fondest thanks to Leslie Stoker, publisher and muse. It has been an honor working with Leslie and everyone at Stewart, Tabori & Chang.

La Bohème

Foreword

A PERFORMANCE OF *LA SYLPHIDE*, with the requisite sylphlike ballerina poised for seemingly inhuman flight, seldom conjures up thoughts of Pasta Bolognese, unless the viewer is wishing it for the dancer in a moment of nutritional altruism. Nor do the opening lines of Beethoven's Fifth Symphony necessarily make one desire sachertorte. But the opera? There, gastronomic daydreams are almost expected, for no other art form is linked to food and eating to such a colossal degree. Consider the amount of actual eating that occurs on stage, in scenes such as *Don Giovanni's* banquet, a pure expression of decadence and a symbol for the immoral gluttony that brings him to his end; or Falstaff's consumption, which isn't the type that fells Mimi and Violetta; or Massenet's and Charpentier's hearty *verismo* meals, which serve as a backdrop for larger-than-life emotions set in music. After all that drama, sometimes all we really want is the simple glass of water carried down the stairs in the final scene of *Arabella*.

I have often contemplated what it would be like to take part in an authentic, extended Baroque performance at which the audience actually conversed with one another and ate a full dinner during the course of an opera. Being pragmatic, I imagine that the smells of roasted leg of lamb or sautéed foie gras wafting up to the stage, accompanied by clinks of crystal and silverware, would cause salivation very useful for optimal singing.

Such a tradition continues, albeit with far more respect for the artists, in festivals such as Glyndebourne and Bayreuth, where long breaks are taken for leisurely meals between acts. At Glyndebourne, I remember the bucolic image of audience members dressed in their finest, picnicking with a full dinner service and staff on the verdant lawns, with sheep and loping lambs punctuating the fields in the distance. Like Leporello, I was all too tempted to contemplate stealing scraps from the table, but instead I munched on my Stilton cheese and chutney sandwich, accompanied, of course, by strong English tea.

The association between specific dishes and singers, composers, and even operas is equally compelling. Who hasn't relished a Bellini (too often, perhaps?), Tournedos Rossini, Pasta alla Norma, Peach Melba, Chicken Tetrazzini, or my own La Diva Renée, a pastry created by chef Daniel Boulud? Sadly, the era of the truffle-eating, chaise-lounging diva is long gone. Today's singer remains *sempre libera* only if she spends hours at the gym working toward a Hollywood-hard body, Melba toast in hand.

I love the fact that these dishes have entered the larger fabric of our culture, even if few partakers still remember who Nellie Melba, Luisa Tetrazzini, or even Bellini and Rossini were. I'm proud to be part of a tradition that celebrates art and history—*we* remember. Enjoy these and more creative relationships between opera and food while whipping up the delights in this cookbook. *Vissi d'arte, vissi d'amore, viva mangiare!*

RENÉE FLEMING

Introduction

OPERA LOVERS ARE NOT LIKE OTHER PEOPLE. They are unabashed in their passion, deliriously immersing themselves in opera's rich outpouring of melody, emotion, and theatricality. In fact, almost no enthusiast on the planet embraces sensual pleasure more deeply than the opera lover . . .

. . . unless it's the gourmet. Like opera lovers, food connoisseurs will go to extreme lengths to indulge their passion, gladly driving fifty miles for perfect heirloom tomatoes or spending an entire weekend preparing a sauce reduction.

When the opera lover and the food lover turn up in the same person (and it happens surprisingly often), the result tends to be the "compleat aesthete," someone of urgent yet refined appetites, an epicure of all five senses: the sights and sounds of Grand Opera; the taste, smell, and feel of Grand Food. If you could hear a delicious meal or taste a great performance, this delightful nexus might not exist. But as it stands, opera and food are complementary passions that add up to much more than the sum of their parts. And their happy affinity is why *Opera Lover's Cookbook* came to be.

It has been said that every great opera conjures its own unique universe. Similarly, I believe that every great dinner party is a once-in-a-lifetime coming together of guest list, menu, setting, décor, time, and theme. You, the hostess or host, are the principal conjurer of this magical event, the conceiver and producer of an entertainment happening that can never be fully controlled but only guided and presided over.

In creating *Opera Lover's Cookbook*, my fondest wish is that the intense pleasure I've taken in imagining, preparing, refining, and sharing these menus will serve to spur your own imaginings as you plan your meal. And I'm hoping that the many glorious worlds of Grand Opera that have inspired me will resonate with you and transform your special evening into an utterly enchanting moment in time.

Perhaps your occasion will share the reckless gaiety of Violetta's Act I soirée. Or maybe you'll feel the youthful excitement of sitting with Bohemian friends at the Café Momus. Or your meal may have the charming bread-and-cheese simplicity of Cavaradossi's picnic basket. Who knows? I hope you'll see the menus in this book as an imaginative blueprint to work from as you dream up many sensuous, pleasure-filled and, above all, passionate evenings of merry togetherness.

FRANCINE SEGAN

Chapter One

Bel Canto Elegant Five-Course Dinner

A lieto convito,

To the merry banquet,

amici, v'invito

friends, I invite you

L'ELISIR D'AMORE

BEL CANTO OPERA inspires this elegant five-course meal celebrating the works of early-nineteenth-century Italian composers Gioacchino Antonio Rossini, Gaetano Donizetti, and Vincenzo Bellini. Some of these recipes date back to their lifetimes, such as Penne alla *Norma*, named after Bellini's beloved opera *Norma*, and Tournedos Rossini, a dish combining the maestro's favorite ingredients—foie gras and truffles. Other recipes are classic dishes from their hometowns, such as Bittersweet Chocolate Rice Pudding from Bellini's birthplace in Sicily and an assortment of cheese appetizers from Donizetti's native region of Lombardy.

Like good music, this menu has a theme. Mediterranean fruits accent the cocktails; add highlights to the appetizers and main course; and spice the desserts, carrying the motif to its delicious conclusion. Although extensive, the menu can be prepared by one person in a few hours, as it contains many easy-to-make or make-ahead recipes like the fragrant and delicious Golden Marsala Broth. The menu is arranged as a sit-down dinner with five courses, starting with predinner cocktails and nibbles. Of course, you can omit or combine courses as you please. You might skip the soup course or do all five without the appetizers. No matter how you shift or rearrange the dishes, you'll eventually want to try them all. I predict that, just like Rossini's operas, these recipes will become cherished staples in your repertoire.

Menu

COCKTAILS

William Tell *Apple Martini*   *Bellini Martini*

William Tell *Act III*   *L'Elisir d'Amore*

Classic Bellini

APPETIZERS

Dates with Gorgonzola Dolce Latte

Taleggio with Vincotto

Bel Paese with Hot Pepper Marmalade

Figs with Mascarpone

Tournedos Rossini

FIRST COURSE

Golden Marsala Broth

SECOND COURSE

Penne alla Norma

MAIN COURSE

L'Italiana in Algeri *Couscous with Fiery Chicken*

Sautéed Broccoli Rabe with Red Pepper Garlic Crisps

SALAD COURSE

Salad of Autumn Hues with Rossini's Truffle Dressing

DESSERT

Bittersweet Chocolate Rice Pudding

Sugar and Spice Ricotta Cheesecake

AFTER-DINNER DRINK

Cream di Limoncella

PREVIOUS PAGES: *L'Elisir d'Amore*

Cocktails

A GOOD RULE OF THUMB for a gathering of eight to twelve guests is to offer two mixed cocktails as well as wine and sparkling water. Most guests, when offered a "house" cocktail, opt for that instead of wine, so be sure to plan accordingly. Set out the drinks so that guests can help themselves. You'll need: ice; glasses; cocktail napkins; a plate of lemon or lime wedges; bottles of sparkling water or a nonalcoholic cocktail; red and white wine and a wine opener; and two "house cocktails," pre-mixed and served in cocktail shakers or pitchers.

WILLIAM TELL APPLE MARTINI
Serves 1

Guests at the premiere gala of Rossini's opera *William Tell*—Paris, 1829—were served apple tarts, each topped with an apple pierced by a sugar arrow. Here's a liquid version.

> 1 ounce Citadelle Apple Vodka
> 1 ounce apple schnapps such as Apple Pucker
> ½ ounce Triple Sec
> ½ ounce lemon-lime soda
> 1 Lady apple or green apple slice, for garnish

Combine the vodka, schnapps, Triple Sec, soda, and crushed ice in a shaker and mix well. Strain into a chilled martini glass. Garnish with a small Lady apple or apple slice.

WILLIAM TELL ACT III
Serves 1

Mini Pommes au Calvados, baby apples in brandy sold in glass jars in gourmet grocers, are a delicious and gorgeous garnish for this cocktail.

> 1 ounce Calvados
> 2 ounces sparkling apple cider
> 1 mini Pomme au Calvados, for garnish

Pour the Calvados into a chilled martini glass and top with cider. Garnish with a brandied mini apple.

CLASSIC BELLINI
Serves 1

The Bellini, first created in the 1930s at Harry's Bar in Venice, was actually named for the Renaissance painter Giovanni Bellini, not Vincenzo Bellini, the bel canto composer. Instead of peach puree, try peach liqueur for a twist on the classic.

> 1 peach
> 3 ounces champagne or Prosecco

Peel the peach and puree it in a food processor until very liquidy. Place 1 tablespoon of the peach puree into the bottom of a chilled champagne flute and top with champagne.

"To eat, to love, to sing, and to digest; in truth, these are the four acts in this opera buffa that we call life, and which vanish like the bubbles in a bottle of champagne."

GIOACCHINO ROSSINI

OPERA NOTE

Rossini drew little pictures of wine bottles in the margins of letters to friends to express his disappointment with an opera performance. The worse he felt things went, the more wine bottles he drew. Why draw wine bottles?

The Italian word for a wine bottle is *fiasco*, a term that in early-nineteenth-century Italy came to be associated with a theatrical failure. According to one legend, this originated when audience members would heckle performers by noisily blowing across the tops of their wine bottles. The term more likely comes from the fact that Venetian glass blowers converted their mistakes into cheap wine bottles. The word *fiasco* came to be associated with any sort of mistake or shoddy workmanship.

PROSECCO

Prosecco, popular in Italy, is still relatively uncommon here in the States. Introduce this sparkling wine to your friends. They'll enjoy its small bubbles, lovely fruit aroma, and crisp refreshing taste. And unlike true French Champagne, superb Prosecco can be had at reasonable prices.

Prosecco is the name of the wine as well as the name of the grape used to make it. Many of the best examples of Prosecco are, not surprisingly, made of 100 percent Prosecco grape.

Prosecco is wonderful served icy cold in a chilled champagne flute, but it also pairs well with a surprisingly long list of ingredients. Try it with a touch of aromatic syrup such as lavender, rose, or violet (see page 210 for sources); a splash of pomegranate juice or elderflower soda; or an ounce of limoncella or other citrus liqueur.

BELLINI MARTINI
Serves 1

Stronger than a traditional Bellini, but still light and refreshing.

- **2 ounces peach vodka**
- **1 ounce peach nectar**
- **Splash of peach liqueur**
- **1 peach slice, for garnish**

Combine the vodka, nectar, liqueur, and crushed ice in a shaker and mix well. Strain into a chilled martini glass and garnish with a peach slice.

L'ELISIR D'AMORE
Serves 1

Dulcamara's supposedly magical elixir was really only Bordeaux wine. This unusual cocktail uses Elisir du Dr. Roux, a bright green liqueur made with a dozen herbs and aromatics. While not exactly magical either, it is certainly enchanting.

- **1 ounce freshly squeezed orange juice**
- **1/2 ounce Elisir du Dr. Roux**
- **1/2 ounce sweet vermouth**
- **1 orange slice, for garnish**

Combine the juice, Elisir, vermouth, and crushed ice in a shaker and mix well. Strain into a chilled old-fashioned or short glass and garnish with an orange slice.

Appetizers

The issue of whether or not you should assign seats at a dinner party has been debated since the time of Socrates. Truly.

Ancient philosophers argued the issue, with some contending that guests could best decide for themselves where to sit and would be happiest if the individual were in charge of his own seating destiny. Others advocated assigned seating, stressing that only the host knew everyone and could best balance dinner partners so conversation flowed smoothly. Another argument for assigned seating was the fact that guests of higher rank must be properly honored with the best seat, which could only be guaranteed if the host took charge.

I always assign seats. I seat by personality style rather than profession. I've studied up on my ancient Greek and taken to heart the seventh-century BC poet Hesiod's advice not to seat people in the same profession together, "for beggar is jealous of beggar and bard of bard." The first-century historian Plutarch advised to "separate contentious, abusive, and quick-tempered men by placing between them some easy-going men as a cushion to soften their clashing," so I'm always careful to put an introvert near an extrovert and a mellow, carefree person near someone more intense.

CHEESES OF DONIZETTI'S LOMBARDY

Donizetti came from the Lombardy region of Italy, famous for its wonderful cheeses, which include:

BEL PAESE—which means "beautiful country," a mild, soft, butter-yellow cow's milk cheese.

BRANZI—a mix of cow's and goat's milk.

CRESCENZA—a mild cow's milk cheese with the consistency of butter.

GORGONZOLA—the best comes from the town of Gorgonzola—a cow's milk blue cheese with green-colored striations called "veins." Select the delicious Gorgonzola dolce latte, sweet milk Gorgonzola.

MASCARPONE—a cow's milk cheese with a soft, buttery consistency that can substitute for whipped cream as a topping.

ROBIOLA—a runny, rich, and creamy cow's milk cheese; ROBIOLINA is a stronger-tasting version of robiola.

TALEGGIO—a semisoft cow's milk cheese that has a subtle taste; TALEGGINO is its slightly stronger-tasting relative.

"Appetite is for the stomach what love is for the heart. The stomach is the conductor, who rules the grand orchestra of our passions, and rouses it to action."

GIOACCHINO ROSSINI

Luciano Pavarotti in *L'Elisir d'Amore*

SET DESIGN

Arrange the cheese on a large wooden cutting board, on a slab of marble, or in a wicker basket lined with grape leaves.

You can put out standard cheese knives or indulge your fancy and set out an assortment of amusing cheese knives found in specialty stores, flea markets, or antique stores.

Serve the cheese with small clusters of grapes, clementine sections, fresh kumquats, red currants, Lady apples, or Seckel pears. Add a variety of nuts in their shells, along with nutcrackers and small bowls for shells. Walnuts, Brazil nuts, almonds, and hazelnuts create especially nice color and size contrasts. Add breadsticks and crisp raw veggies arranged in vases. Decorate the serving platter with dried bay leaves or fresh herbs, as is done in Italy.

DATES WITH GORGONZOLA DOLCE LATTE
Serves 8

The naturally sweet taste and silky texture of dates blends wonderfully with tangy Gorgonzola. Like gifted coloratura sopranos, these nibbles hit a high note with no stridency. Be warned: they are dangerously addictive, even to those who think they don't like Gorgonzola.

> **16 dates (select soft dates with unwrinkled skins)**
> **2 ounces Gorgonzola dolce latte cheese**
> **1 clementine**
> **20 whole almonds, shelled**

Slit the dates partway down the middle and remove the pits. Using a small spoon, fill each date with Gorgonzola. Zest the clementine and reserve the zest. Peel the clementine and divide it into segments.

Arrange the Gorgonzola-dates on a serving platter with the clementine segments and almonds. Garnish with the clementine zest.

TALEGGIO WITH VINCOTTO
Serves 8

Vincotto is a tangy-sweet, thick condiment made from vine-dried grapes gently simmered and then aged in oak barrels. An amazingly versatile product, it tastes a little like aged balsamic vinegar, but richer and sweeter. It is well worth the trip to a specialty gourmet shop or Web site. It is stupendous with cheese and adds rich and complex flavors to simple grilled vegetables, fish, and meats. Once you taste it, you'll wonder how you ever got along without it. (See page 210 for online sources of this delectable treat.)

> **8 ounces Taleggio or other mild Lombardy cheese such as Bel Paese**
> **8 strawberries, stems on**
> **1 ounce vincotto or best-quality aged balsamic vinegar**

Cut the cheese into bite-sized cubes. Skewer each with an attractive cocktail toothpick. Arrange the cheese and strawberries on a plate. Serve the vincotto in a tiny bowl or shot glass for dipping. Encourage guests to dip the strawberries also.

BEL PAESE WITH HOT PEPPER MARMALADE
Serves 8

Pop this gorgeous appetizer in your mouth and be prepared to swoon.

First you'll experience the sweet heat of the hot pepper marmalade, next the buttery richness of the cheese, and finally the chewy tang of dried guava. They are irresistible, so be sure to make a lot!

You'll need two specialty items—hot pepper marmalade and dried guava slices—but I promise that both will become pantry staples, so make the effort to find them. You won't be disappointed. (See page 210 for a list of online sources for these versatile products.)

In a pinch, instead of guava slices you can use bite-sized sections of apricot fruit leather, available in most super-markets.

> **6 to 8 large slices dried guava**
>
> **4 ounces Bel Paese or Taleggio cheese**
>
> **1 ounce hot pepper marmalade or red pepper jelly**
>
> **3 to 5 jalapeño peppers as garnish, optional**

Cut the guava slices into bite-sized sections and top each with a portion of cheese and a dollop of marmalade. Arrange the slices on a serving platter and, if you like, decorate with fresh jalapeños.

OPERA NOTE

Beverly Sills, a renowned interpreter of the bel canto repertoire, used her endearing nickname, "Bubbles," for the title of her memoirs. Sills debuted in the Met's premiere production of Rossini's *The Siege of Corinth* in 1975 and went on to serve as chairman of the Met from 2002 to 2005, helping to raise millions of dollars in funds for new productions and the Saturday afternoon broadcasts.

The last role Ms. Sills ever performed at the Met was Norina in Donizetti's *Don Pasquale* in 1979, a part she called a "cream-puff role" that could be handled easily.

Marilyn Horne and Fernando Corena in *L'Italiana in Algeri*

FIGS WITH MASCARPONE
Serves 6

Here's a neat trick that lets you enjoy summer-sweet figs any time of year. Just simmer dried figs in white wine for a few minutes until they plump up.

Topped with creamy mascarpone cheese and a gorgeous sprinkle of pistachios, this is an elegant and simple-to-make appetizer.

- **18 whole dried figs**
- **1 cup white wine**
- **2 ounces mascarpone cheese**
- **2 tablespoons finely chopped pistachio nuts**

Bring the figs and wine to a simmer in a saucepan over low heat until the figs are soft, about 5 minutes. Remove the figs with a slotted spoon and allow to cool.

Cut ¼ inch off the tops of the figs and set them, cut side up, onto a serving platter. Top the figs with a dollop of mascarpone and a sprinkle of pistachios.

Bella vita! Oh, che bel piacere!

What a lovely life! Oh, what a pleasure!

Io di più non so bramar.

I couldn't wish for more.

Pappataci dee mangiar,

Pappataci just has to eat,

Pappataci dee dormir.

Pappataci just has to sleep.

L'ITALIANA IN ALGERI

OPERA NOTE

Although he lived another forty years,
Rossini stopped composing operas after
his thirty-seventh birthday. In his later years,
he wrote piano pieces, including one
whimsically entitled "Radishes, Anchovy,
Pickles, Butter, Dry Figs, Almonds,
Raisins, and Hazelnuts."

TOURNEDOS ROSSINI
Serves 6 to 8

This dish was served as a main course in Rossini's day. The flavors are so powerfully decadent that I prefer serving appetizer-sized portions.

- 1 small fresh truffle, black or white
- 4 ounces foie gras, cut into 3 slices
- Salt and freshly milled black pepper
- ½ cup Madeira
- 1 filet mignon steak, about 6 to 7 ounces
- 1 tablespoon extra-virgin olive oil
- 1 tablespoon unsalted butter, plus more as needed
- 6 to 8 slices best-quality white bread

Place three-quarters of the truffle, thinly sliced, into a shallow dish. Reserve the remaining truffle section for garnish. Season the foie gras with salt and pepper. Place the foie gras over the truffles and add the Madeira. Cover and marinate for 15 minutes.

Meanwhile, season the filet generously with salt and pepper. Add the oil to a small sauté pan, and over high heat, sear the filet for 3 to 4 minutes per side. Remove it from the pan and reserve, covered, to keep warm. Wipe the pan with a paper towel.

Remove the foie gras from the marinade. Reserve the truffles and Madeira.

In the sauté pan, melt 1 tablespoon of the butter over medium-high heat and add the foie gras. Sear for 1 to 2 minutes per side, adding more butter if necessary. Remove the foie gras and reserve.

Pour the reserved Madeira and truffles into the pan and combine with the foie gras juices. Cook the sauce for about 5 minutes until reduced by half. Season with salt and pepper.

Slice the filet mignon vertically into thin slices. Cut the foie gras into small sections. Toast the bread slices, then lightly butter them. Trim away the crusts and cut the slices into bite-sized sections.

To serve, place the toasts onto a serving platter and top each with a slice of filet, a drizzle of Madeira-truffle sauce, and the foie gras slice. Grate the reserved truffle over the top. Serve immediately.

OPERA NOTE

Rossini's delight in foie gras and truffles was so legendary that the world-class chefs of his day, such as Auguste Escoffier and Marie-Antoine Carême, created dozens of dishes in his honor using those ingredients. Tournedos Rossini, probably the most famous, is filet mignon topped with foie gras and truffles served on toast. It was concocted by a French chef at one of the composer's favorite dining spots, Café Anglais in Paris.

Here's one legend about how the dish got its name. The chef preparing the filet mignon became so exasperated at Rossini's constant culinary micromanaging that he shouted his protest at the maestro. Undaunted, Rossini shouted back, *"Et alors, tournez le dos!"*—So, turn your back!

"Tournez le dos" supposedly became tournedos.

COSTARS IN THE KITCHEN

Select one of your guests to costar with you in the kitchen. Don't be shy about soliciting help. The guest will feel honored to have been asked.

Either you or your costar chef should make Tournedos Rossini at the last minute so it can be served hot.

First Course: Soup

BECOME A NUTMEG SNOB. Use only freshly grated nutmeg. It's actually better to omit the nutmeg rather than use ready-ground.

Nutmeg was so stylish in eighteenth- and nineteenth-century high society that all distinguished ladies and gentlemen carried personal-sized graters. These finely crafted pocket-sized graters came in whimsical shapes such as a lute, acorn, Rococo-style urn, and even a nutmeg itself. They accompanied the aristocracy everywhere, even to formal dinner parties and fine restaurants.

For collectors these antique nutmeg grinders make gorgeous tabletop decorations and are wonderful conversation starters!

GOLDEN MARSALA BROTH
Serves 4

Don't underestimate this marvelous recipe just because it's simple to prepare. Yes, it has only a few ingredients, and yes, it takes only minutes to make, but your guests won't know that.

The key is Marsala, that delightful golden alcohol-fortified wine from Sicily, the birthplace of Vincenzo Bellini. Marsala adds a wonderfully rich taste.

The velvety smooth soup is infused with the irresistible aroma of nutmeg and cinnamon, which brings to mind cozy fireplaces and good music.

4 egg yolks

2 cups best-quality chicken stock

3 tablespoons Marsala

3 tablespoons unsalted butter

¼ teaspoon cinnamon

½ teaspoon sugar

Salt and freshly milled black pepper

Freshly grated nutmeg

Fresh thyme, optional

In a medium saucepan, over low heat, whisk the yolks, stock, and Marsala until creamy smooth.

Simmer the mixture, whisking constantly, until warm. Do not bring the soup to a boil or the yolks will curdle.

Once the soup has reached the desired serving temperature, whisk in the butter, cinnamon, sugar, and salt and pepper to taste.

Serve topped with a pinch of freshly grated nutmeg and a sprinkle of thyme, if using.

OPERA NOTE

Rossini claims to have cried only three times in his life: the first after a disastrous opera premiere, the second when he heard Niccolo Paganini play the violin, and the third when a picnic basket containing his favorite dish, turkey stuffed with truffles, fell overboard during a boat outing.

Second Course: Pasta

RICOTTA, WHICH MEANS "recooked" in Italian, is common to us in the United States. However, many of ricotta's relatives are virtual unknowns.

Ricotta salata is semifirm and very flavorful. Its mild, salty taste makes it especially wonderful as a topping for fish. Ricotta secca, even firmer, is perfect for grating in place of Parmesan or Romano cheese. Ricotta infornata, Sicilian-style brown-baked ricotta, is delicious plain or as a rich topping for cooked pasta, meat, or vegetable dishes. Ricotta forte, almost impossible to locate in the States, is found throughout Italy's Apulia region. It is a double-fermented ricotta with a sharp, pungent flavor that's indescribably good—a must-try on your next visit to southern Italy.

> "Two lines only, O my dear friend, to give you word about my health, which is at the breaking point from the great fatigue that I am experiencing because of having to compose the opera in a short time, and whose fault is that? That of my usual and original poet, the God of Sloth!"
>
> **VINCENZO BELLINI**

PENNE ALLA *NORMA*
Serves 4 to 6

This oniony-sweet Sicilian-style tomato sauce brings out the smoky undertones of the eggplant, while the tangy ricotta salata provides just the right finish.

This traditional Sicilian pasta dish, renamed back in Bellini's day in homage to his opera *Norma*, is a definite crowd-pleaser.

- 4 small or 3 medium eggplants, skins on, cut into 1-inch pieces
- Kosher salt
- 1/2 cup all-purpose flour
- 1/2 cup extra-virgin olive oil, plus more as needed
- 1 large Vidalia onion, sliced
- 4 cloves garlic, minced
- 2 1/2 pounds plum tomatoes, peeled, seeded, and chopped (or one 28-ounce can best-quality crushed tomatoes, drained)
- 2 tablespoons sugar
- Salt and freshly milled black pepper
- 1 pound penne
- 1/2 cup ricotta salata, coarsely grated
- 12 large fresh basil leaves
- Red pepper flakes

Sprinkle the eggplant cubes with kosher salt and place them in a colander. Set the colander in the sink and allow the eggplant to drain for 20 minutes. Pat well with paper towels to remove all excess moisture.

Toss the eggplant with the flour.

Heat ¼ cup of the oil in a large nonstick skillet over medium-high heat. Cook the eggplant in batches so the pieces fry without crowding. Fry each batch until golden brown on all sides, about 5 minutes per batch. Remove the eggplant with a slotted spoon and transfer to a paper-towel-lined plate to drain.

In a large, heavy-bottomed pot, heat the remaining ¼ cup of oil over medium heat. Add the onion, cover, and stirring occasionally, cook for about 15 minutes, until very soft. Remove the cover. Add the garlic and continue cooking until softened, about 2 minutes. Stir in the tomatoes and sugar. Season to taste with salt and pepper. Cook covered for about 15 minutes.

While cooking the onions, bring a large pot of salted water to a boil. Add the penne and cook according to the package directions. Drain.

To serve, spoon the sauce onto the penne and top with eggplant, ricotta salata, basil leaves, and a sprinkle of red pepper flakes.

Joan Sutherland and Marilyn Horne in *Norma*

Main Course

DINING SCENES PLAY A PART IN MANY OF ROSSINI'S OPERAS, including *La Cambiale di Matrimonio, Il Viaggio a Reims,* and *Ciro in Babilonia.*

Perhaps the most amusing food scene in all of opera occurs in *L'Italiana in Algeri,* when the Italian Isabella distracts Mustafà, her Algerian captor, with the nuances of spaghetti-twirling so she can make her escape.

L'ITALIANA IN ALGERI COUSCOUS WITH FIERY CHICKEN
Serves 4 to 6

Couscous, an ingredient in both Sicilian and Algerian cuisine, is the perfect dish to celebrate *L'Italiana in Algeri.* Seasoned with aromatic spice market favorites like cardamom, nutmeg, cloves, and saffron, the fruit- and tomato-studded couscous smells so good your knees will go weak.

The pepper-crusted chicken adds just the right heat to the sweet couscous. This is a bold dish to honor Isabella's brassy bravery.

4 to 6 boneless chicken breasts, about 6 ounces each

Salt and coarse black pepper

6 tablespoons extra-virgin olive oil

Freshly squeezed juice of 1 lemon

1 large Vidalia onion, minced

6 or 7 threads saffron

4 cloves garlic, minced

2 stalks celery, plus inner leaves, minced

2 ounces golden raisins

1 pound ripe plum tomatoes, peeled, seeded, and chopped (or one 14.5-ounce can of diced tomatoes, drained)

1½ cups best-quality chicken stock

1 bunch flat-leaf parsley, leaves only, minced

2 bay leaves

¼ teaspoon ground cloves

¼ teaspoon ground cardamom

6 to 7 whole allspice, or ¼ teaspoon ground allspice

One 2-inch stick of cinnamon

Freshly squeezed juice and zest of 1 orange

1½ cups couscous

Freshly grated nutmeg

Red pepper flakes

Lemon wedges, for garnish

Season the chicken with salt and lots of black pepper. Heat 3 tablespoons of the oil in a large skillet over medium-high heat. Use a heavy lid or foil-covered brick to press down the chicken and sauté the chicken until browned on one side. Turn the chicken over, top with the lemon juice, and sauté until no pink remains. Reserve the chicken, covered, on a plate.

In the same skillet, add the remaining 3 tablespoons of oil and sauté the onion and saffron until the onion is golden, 10 to 12 minutes. Add the garlic, celery, and raisins and sauté for 1 minute.

Add the tomatoes, stock, half of the parsley, the bay leaves, cloves, cardamom, allspice, cinnamon, and orange juice and bring to a boil. Reduce heat and simmer, covered, for 10 minutes.

Add the couscous, stirring to dissolve any lumps. Remove from the heat, cover, and let rest 10 minutes, then stir in the orange zest, nutmeg, and salt and pepper to taste. Remove the bay leaves and cinnamon stick.

To serve, arrange the couscous on a platter, top with the chicken, and sprinkle with red pepper flakes. Garnish with lemon wedges and the remaining parsley.

Salad Course

SAUTÉED BROCCOLI RABE WITH RED PEPPER GARLIC CRISPS
Serves 4 to 8

Broccoli rabe, mellowed by a quick sauté in stock, gets a fortissimo crunch from the fiery garlic crisps. A perfect Sicilian side dish—or toss it with cooked spaghetti to make a light main-course supper.

> 3 tablespoons olive oil
>
> ½ teaspoon red pepper flakes
>
> 6 to 8 cloves garlic, thinly sliced
>
> 3 bunches broccoli rabe, cleaned and trimmed
>
> ¼ cup best-quality vegetable or chicken stock
>
> Salt

In a large nonstick skillet, warm the oil and red pepper flakes over medium-high heat. Add the garlic and sauté until golden. Transfer the garlic crisps to a paper towel to drain.

Raise the heat to high. Add the broccoli rabe and sauté for about 1 minute. Add the stock and cover. Simmer until the broccoli rabe is tender but still firm, about 3 minutes. Season with salt to taste. Serve topped with the garlic crisps.

> *"The truffle is the Mozart of mushrooms."*
>
> **GIOACCHINO ROSSINI**

IT'S EASY TO MAKE YOUR OWN TRUFFLE OIL: Combine eight ounces of best-quality olive oil with one black truffle and store in an airtight container for at least four days. You'll create fragrant oil and still be able to use the truffle in another dish.

SALAD OF AUTUMN HUES WITH ROSSINI'S TRUFFLE DRESSING
Serves 6

Dazzle your guests with the beauty of this delicious salad, which displays the splendid colors of fall foliage. The vinaigrette is Rossini's own recipe and is outstanding even when truffles are not in season.

> ¾ cup Provençal olive oil
>
> 2 tablespoons freshly squeezed lemon juice
>
> 2 to 3 tablespoons French Champagne vinegar
>
> ¼ teaspoon Coleman's English prepared mustard
>
> 1 black truffle, finely sliced
>
> Salt and freshly milled black pepper
>
> 2 cups baby greens, such as beet leaves and frisée
>
> 2 cups raw mixed red lobster, orange chanterelle, and yellow hedgehog mushrooms

Whisk the oil, lemon juice, vinegar, and mustard in a small bowl until well blended. Add the truffle and season to taste with salt and pepper.

Arrange the greens on the serving plates. Top each plate with an assortment of mushrooms and drizzle with dressing. Spoon a few slices of truffle from the dressing onto each plate.

Dessert

BITTERSWEET CHOCOLATE RICE PUDDING
Serves 8

Bittersweet chocolate and zesty orange transform rice pudding into something celestial. Creamy and chocolaty with a hint of tangy orange, this easy-to-prepare dessert, called *riso nero*—black rice—in Italy, is a Sicilian creation.

1 cup white rice

Pinch of salt

2 ounces best-quality bittersweet chocolate (at least 70% cacao), cut into small pieces, plus 1 tablespoon shaved, for garnish

¼ cup sugar

1 teaspoon vanilla extract

1 teaspoon freshly grated nutmeg

2 cups heavy cream

Zest of 1 orange

Orange liqueur, such as Cointreau

Combine the rice, salt, and 6 cups of water in a large saucepan over medium-high heat. Boil, uncovered, until the rice is tender but still firm, about 15 minutes. Drain the rice in a colander and return it to the saucepan.

Add the chocolate pieces, sugar, vanilla, and nutmeg and stir until the chocolate is completely dissolved. Add 1½ cups of the cream and the orange zest to the rice, stir, and simmer for about 10 minutes over low heat. Allow to cool to lukewarm, then stir in the orange liqueur to taste. Whip the remaining ½ cup cream until stiff.

Serve the rice pudding immediately, topped with a dollop of whipped cream and a sprinkle of the shaved chocolate.

SUGAR AND SPICE RICOTTA CHEESECAKE
Serves 8

This spicy-sweet ricotta cheesecake is baked and served in tiny pumpkins. If baby pumpkins aren't available, the pudding can easily be made in ramekins or a single springform pan.

A true *finale ultimo*, this dessert always gets rave reviews.

8 mini pumpkins, about 4 inches in diameter

4 large eggs

1½ pounds whole-milk ricotta

1½ cups heavy cream

½ cup sugar, plus more as needed

1 teaspoon freshly grated nutmeg

½ teaspoon ground allspice

¼ teaspoon ground cinnamon

¼ teaspoon ground cloves

¼ teaspoon ground cardamom

3 tablespoons nut liqueur, such as Frangelico

Cut the top off the pumpkins, being careful to keep the stems intact. Reserve the top sections. Scoop out and discard the seeds.

Preheat the oven to 350°F.

In a large bowl, using an electric mixer, beat the eggs until frothy, about 2 minutes. Add the ricotta, ½ cup of the cream, ½ cup of the sugar, and all the spices and beat until very smooth.

Pour the batter into the pumpkin bottoms (or put all the batter into a 9-inch springform pan) and bake, without the lids, on a cookie sheet for about 40 minutes, or about 50 minutes if using a 9-inch pan, until the pudding is set. Allow the pumpkins to cool slightly on a wire rack.

In the bowl of an electric mixer, whip the remaining cup of cream with a dash of sugar until thick. Stir in the nut liqueur.

Top the pudding with a dollop of whipped cream.

After-Dinner Drink

CREAM DI LIMONCELLA
Serves 4

Limoncella, a liqueur from Sicily and the Amalfi coast, is even better served creamed. It's like liquid lemon ice cream.

- 1 cup heavy cream
- 1 vanilla bean
- 4 ounces limoncella liqueur

In a small saucepan, simmer the cream and vanilla bean over low heat for 10 minutes. Cover and allow the cream to cool. Remove the vanilla bean.

Pour the vanilla-cream and limoncella into a sealed glass container. Store in the freezer until ready to serve.

> *"The bassoon or the piccolo, grumbling its discontent or shrilling its longing, personify the empty stomach for me. The stomach replete, on the other hand, is the triangle of enjoyment or the kettle-drum of joy."*
>
> **GIOACCHINO ROSSINI**

Sarò zeppo e contornato
I will have lots of

di memorie e petizioni
memoranda and petitions

di galline e di storioni
of hens and sturgeons

di bottiglie di broccati
of bottles and brocades

di candele e marinati
of candles and marinades

di ciambelle e pasticceti
of buns and cakes

di canditi e di confetti
of candied fruits and sweets

di piastroni, di dobloni
of slabs and doubloons

di vaniglia e di caffè.
of vanilla and coffee.

LA CENERENTOLA

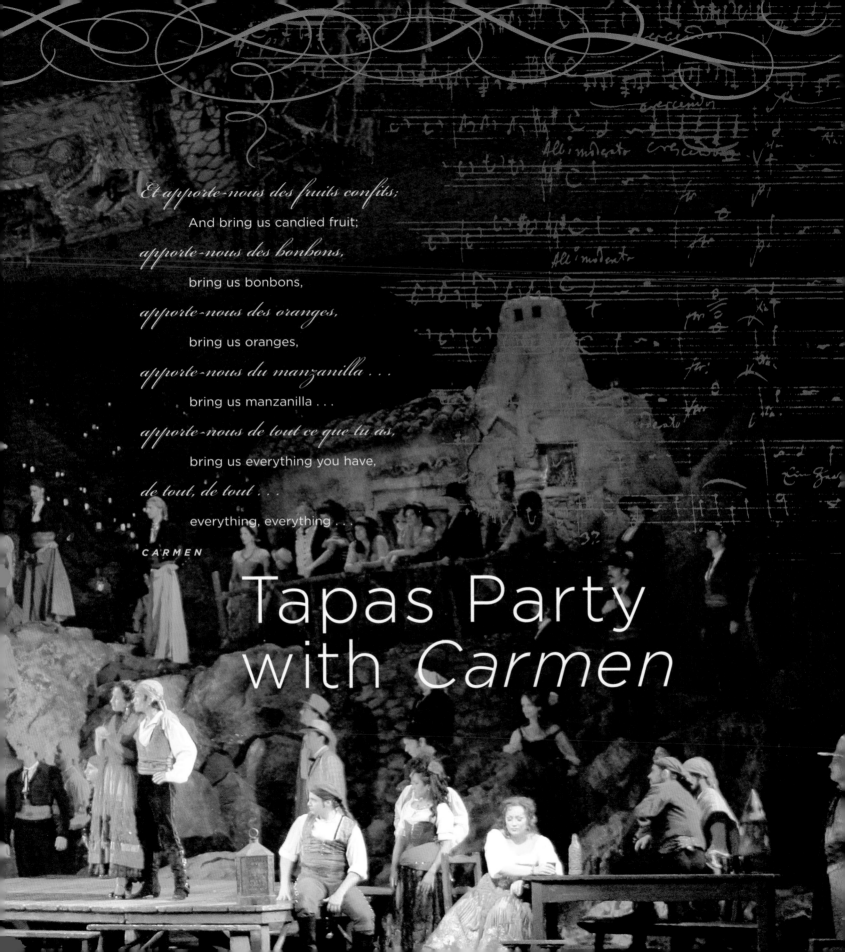

Chapter Two

Et apporte-nous des fruits confits;

And bring us candied fruit;

apporte-nous des bonbons,

bring us bonbons,

apporte-nous des oranges,

bring us oranges,

apporte-nous du manzanilla . . .

bring us manzanilla . . .

apporte-nous de tout ce que tu as,

bring us everything you have,

de tout, de tout . . .

everything, everything . . .

CARMEN

Tapas Party
with *Carmen*

CARMEN IS PLAYING IN THE BACKGROUND. Your friends chat, sipping Spanish sherry. Walking into the room with a plate of Warm Dates with Serrano Ham and Almonds, you shrug off the oohs and aahs, explaining that it took only five minutes to prepare. No one believes you. You smile. ❧

A tapas party is one of the—no, it is *the* easiest way to entertain. Think of it as a meal that skips the main course. Serving nothing but a slew of appetizers makes for an informal, festive atmosphere. A tapas party is an especially good solution for hosting an event in a small space, because everything on the menu is finger food: no dining table, no place settings, no forks or knives are needed. ❧ During your tapas party, play selections from any of the wonderful Spanish-influenced operas such as Bizet's *Carmen*, Rossini's *Il Barbiere di Siviglia*, Verdi's *Don Carlos*, or Mozart's *Don Giovanni*.

Menu

COCKTAILS

Carmen's Sangria

Seville Cocktail

Spanish Gold

Matador

Toreador

Andalusia

TAPAS

Leporello's Chorizo and Potatoes

Saffron Garlic Shrimp

Melted Manchego with Spicy-Sweet Tomato Jam

Serrano Ham with Drunken Melon

Spicy Scallop Seviche

Warm Marinated Olives

Figaro's Fiery Salmon Seviche

Clams with Salsa Verde

Don Giovanni's Octopus with Potatoes

Savory Pork Empanadas

Roasted Pepper and Cheese Empanadas

Warm Dates with Serrano Ham and Almonds

SWEETS

Lime Cilantro Granita

Rose Truffles

Almond Cake Accented with Citrus

Chocolate "Chorizo"

PREVIOUS PAGES: *Carmen*

Cocktails

THE WORLD-RENOWNED BARITONE GERALD FINLEY IS QUITE A WINE AFICIONADO. He muses delightfully and knowledgeably on the subject. In a recent communication with me he wrote, "The wine that Giovanni drinks in the banquet scene in Act II's finale is Marzimino, which was likely to be a rare but highly elegant wine in Mozart and da Ponte's time. The fact that Giovanni could enjoy it in Spain was evidence of his penchant for extravagant living.

"I was pleased to suggest to the props department at the Met that the drink onstage be a teetotaler's concoction of cranberry and grape juices. The result had a good color, wasn't too sweet, and didn't overly stain the costumes. With tapas, of course, Rioja would be the most suitable, and Ribera del Duero is my favorite region."

SPANISH SHERRY

The word *sherry* is an English corruption of Jerez, the town in the Andalusia region of southern Spain that has been making this brandy-fortified wine since the twelfth century.

There are many brands of sherry in each category, so offer a choice of two or three types.

FINO is a dry, pale sherry with a delicate taste and is best served icy cold.

MANZANILLA is an especially dry fino and, like all fino sherry, is best drunk icy cold and when the sherry is young. Manzanilla has a hint of saltiness, so it pairs especially well with seafood.

AMONTILLADO is a mature, aged fino, darker in color and sweeter than a young fino, with a lovely nutty flavor.

OLOROSO is darker and sweeter than either fino or amontillado sherry. It is often called cream, milk, or golden sherry and is drunk at room temperature.

SPANISH WINE

There are hundreds of Spanish wines, such as Penedès, Rais Baixas, Rioja, Somontano, Toro, and Valdepeñas. One of my favorites is Cava, a sparkling white. It's similar to champagne, but softer and fruitier.

Versa il vino. [Beve]

Pour the wine. [Drinks]

Eccelente marzimino!

Marzimino at its best!

DON GIOVANNI

CARMEN'S SANGRIA
Serves 8 to 10

Instead of adding ice, which waters down sangria, make frozen juice cubes. Pomegranate juice is an especially delicious flavor for sangria.

One 750-ml bottle red wine

$3/4$ cup brandy or cognac

$1/4$ cup orange liqueur such as Cointreau

$1/4$ cup freshly squeezed orange juice

$1/4$ cup pomegranate juice

1 cup lemon soda

2 fresh peaches, sliced

1 orange, thinly sliced

1 lemon, thinly sliced

1 lime, thinly sliced

Combine the wine, brandy, liqueur, and juices in a glass pitcher. Stir, then add the lemon soda and fruit. Stir in frozen juice cubes or ice.

Votre toast, je peux vous le rendre,

I can reply to your toast,

Señors, señors, car avec les soldats

Sirs, for the soldier and the bullfighter

Oui, les toreros peuvent s'entendre;

Understand each other;

Pour plaisirs, pour plaisirs, ils ont les combats!

Both take pleasure in combat!

CARMEN

SEVILLE COCKTAIL
Serves 1

$1^1/2$ ounces gin

$1/2$ ounce fino sherry

$1/2$ ounce orange juice

Juice of $1/2$ lemon

$1/2$ teaspoon superfine sugar

Combine the gin, sherry, juices, sugar, and crushed ice in a shaker until well mixed. Pour the cocktail into a chilled old-fashioned glass or wine glass.

SPANISH GOLD
Serves 1

$1^1/2$ ounces gin

$1/2$ ounce red wine

$1/4$ ounce dark rum

$1/2$ ounce orange juice

Slice of lime, for garnish

Combine the gin, wine, rum, juice, and crushed ice in a shaker and shake well. Pour into a chilled martini glass and garnish with a slice of lime.

MATADOR
Serves 1

Coarse salt

Freshly squeezed juice of 1 lime

$1^1/2$ ounces tequila

$1/2$ ounce Triple Sec

Put a little salt into a small bowl. Run a section of lime over the rim of a chilled martini glass and then press the rim into the salt.

Combine the lime juice, tequila, Triple Sec, and crushed ice in a shaker and mix well. Pour into the prepared glass.

TOREADOR
Serves 1

1½ ounces tequila

½ ounce crème de cacao

2 tablespoons heavy cream

Whipped cream, for topping

Cocoa powder, for topping

Combine the tequila, crème de cacao, and cream in a shaker with crushed ice and mix well. Pour into a chilled wine glass and top with a dollop of whipped cream and sprinkle of cocoa.

ANDALUSIA
Serves 1

¾ ounce light rum

¾ ounce brandy

¾ ounce dry sherry

Dash of bitters

Combine the rum, brandy, and sherry in a shaker with crushed ice and mix well. Pour into a chilled wine glass and top with bitters.

Grace Bumbry in *Carmen*

Près des remparts de Séville,

Near the ramparts of Seville

Chez mon ami, Lillas Pastia

At the place of my friend, Lillas Pastia

J'irai danser la Séguedille

I will go to dance the Seguedilla

Et boire du manzanilla.

And to drink manzanilla.

CARMEN

"As a musician I tell you that if you were to suppress adultery, fanaticism, crime, evil, the supernatural, there would no longer be the means for writing one note."

GEORGES BIZET

Tapas

THE WORD *TAPAS* COMES FROM THE SPANISH *TAPAR*, which means "to cover." In Spain barkeepers traditionally served drinks covered, topped with a small plate of complimentary nibbles.

There are many ready-made Spanish tapas delicacies available at gourmet grocers. See page 210 for a list of online sources for foods such as

CHORIZO—a spicy smoked pork sausage. Serve it sliced with thick-cut potato chips or crusty bread.

SERRANO HAM—a dry-cured ham, *jamon*, from Spain with a deeper flavor and coarser texture than Italian prosciutto.

MOJAMA—air-dried fresh tuna loin. Serve it sliced paper-thin with wedges of lemon and crusty bread.

SPANISH OLIVES—large green queen or manzanilla olives, either plain or stuffed with a variety of fillings, including anchovies, garlic, piquillo peppers, salmon, almonds, and onions.

MARCONA ALMONDS—large, flavorful almonds from Valencia served fried in olive oil and topped with sea salt.

CAPER BERRIES—the fruit of the mature caper bud. The olive-sized caper berries come with an attractive long stem and are much, much milder than tiny capers. A wonderful nibble with drinks.

SARDINES OR ANCHOVIES—in many ready-made varieties, such as boquerones, a vinegar-cured anchovy from Cantabria.

OCTOPUS—ready-made sold in either spicy tomato sauce, vinaigrette, or garlic sauce. Be sure to buy octopus packed in olive oil, never vegetable oil, as the flavor is startlingly better. Goya brand, a supermarket staple, makes a delicious canned octopus in garlic sauce.

PIQUILLO PEPPERS—wood-roasted red peppers from Navarra, ready-made in glass jars, available in most gourmet food shops.

MARINATED OR GRILLED VEGETABLES—artichokes, asparagus, mushrooms, onions, and oil-cured sun-dried tomatoes; all make wonderful tapas.

Spain boasts over 100 types of cheeses. Try offering a selection as part of your tapas spread. Traditionally, Spanish cheese is served with a wedge of membrillo—quince paste—or slices of fig-nut log, available in fine cheese shops. Here are a few of my favorites:

CABRALES is a pungent blue cheese made from a blend of cow's, goat's, and sheep's milk, matured in the naturally formed caves of the Pico de Gallo Mountains in northern Spain.

GARROTXA is a hard goat's-milk cheese with a mild, nutty flavor.

IBERICO is a hard cheese that's perfect to eat plain or use for cooking. It's made from a blend of cow, goat, and sheep's milk.

IDIAZABAL is a sweet, smoky aromatic sheep's-milk cheese from Navarra in the Pyrenees.

MAHON is a hard cow's-milk cheese with a sweet, fruity aroma and rich taste. The orange outer rind is colored and flavored with Spanish paprika.

MANCHEGO is a raw sheep's-milk cheese with a slightly salty-nutty flavor, sold both young and aged. It comes from Manchego in La Mancha, of *Don Quixote* fame.

RONCAL is a hard sheep's-milk cheese with fresh herb flavor and aroma.

TETILLA is a rich, smooth, slightly salty cow's-milk cheese, sold in a pear shape, resembling a breast—giving the cheese its name.

LEPORELLO'S CHORIZO AND POTATOES
Serves 4 to 6

Leporello would certainly have gone to great lengths to steal a bite of this warm potato salad with the spicy kick of chorizo and jalapeño and the sweet, smoky flavor of pimentón.

Pimentón, a Spanish paprika made of sun-dried, roasted red peppers, has a richer, sweeter taste than ordinary paprika and will fast become one of your favorite spices.

> 1 large Spanish onion, thinly sliced
>
> 1 jalapeño pepper, seeded and sliced
>
> ¼ cup olive oil
>
> ¾ pound Spanish chorizo sausage, sliced
>
> 2 potatoes, peeled and cut into cubes, about 1 pound
>
> 3 cloves garlic, minced
>
> 1 tablespoon pimentón or sweet smoked paprika
>
> 1 bay leaf
>
> 3 tablespoons chopped fresh parsley leaves, for garnish

In a medium saucepan over medium-high heat, sauté the onion and jalapeño in oil until the onion is golden, about 5 minutes. Add the chorizo, potatoes, garlic, and pimentón and sauté for 5 minutes, until the potatoes begin to color. Add the bay leaf and 1 cup boiling water, cover, and continue cooking until the potatoes are tender, about 10 minutes. Add more water, a little at a time, if needed.

To serve, transfer the potato mixture to a serving bowl and top with parsley.

OPERA NOTE

Don Giovanni offers tapas-like nibbles throughout Act I as a way to divert attention from his philandering. At the wedding party Don Giovanni orders Leporello to instruct the servants to ply Masetto and guests with food and drink, and later, in the "Champagne aria," we hear his whirlwind plans to get everyone drunk so he can slink off with Zerlina. In the finale he and Leporello offer tempting ices and sweets as a distraction.

OPERA NOTE

One of the most amusing food scenes in opera occurs in the last act of *Don Giovanni*. The Don's faithful servant, Leporello, overcome with hunger at watching his master eat, snatches mouthfuls of food when he thinks the Don isn't looking.

Clearly suspicious, the Don repeatedly asks Leporello to sing or whistle. Leporello, his mouth full of food, pretends to have a sore throat and can't oblige.

SAFFRON GARLIC SHRIMP
Serves 4 to 6

Gambas al ajillo, as this dish is called in Spain, is best eaten sizzling hot, when the aroma of the garlic and saffron are most potent. For a dramatic presentation, cook and serve it in a small iron skillet.

> 12 medium shrimp, peeled and deveined
> 4 cloves garlic, thinly sliced
> 3 tablespoons olive oil
> 7 to 8 strands saffron
> 1 jalapeño pepper, sliced
> Salt and freshly milled black pepper

Combine the shrimp, garlic, oil, saffron, and jalapeño in a small bowl. Cover with plastic wrap and refrigerate overnight so the flavors can mingle.

Heat a small skillet over high heat and sauté the shrimp with the marinade until the shrimp are golden, about 3 minutes. Season to taste with salt and pepper.

CLOCKWISE FROM TOP: **Saffron Garlic Shrimp, Spicy-Sweet Tomato Jam, Melted Manchego, Chorizos, Warm Marinated Spanish Olives**

MELTED MANCHEGO WITH SPICY-SWEET TOMATO JAM
Serves 4 to 6

Lovely manchego is melted in a pan with a hint of garlic and then spiked with a splash of sherry. The aromas will drive all the guests straight into the kitchen.

The tomato jam, a spicy-sweet mix of tomatoes, sugar, jalapeño, and lemon, is simple to make yet adds just the right zing to the warm, melty cheese.

> One 14.5-ounce can diced tomatoes
> 3/4 cup sugar
> 1 jalapeño pepper, sliced
> Freshly squeezed juice and zest of 1 lemon
> 1/4 teaspoon salt
> Cayenne, optional
> 1 pound manchego, Garrotxa, or tetilla cheese, or a combination
> 2 tablespoons extra-virgin olive oil
> 2 cloves garlic, thinly sliced
> 1 tablespoon sweet sherry
> Crusty bread, sliced

For the jam, combine the tomatoes, sugar, jalapeño, lemon juice and zest, and salt in a medium saucepan and simmer over medium-low heat for about 30 minutes, until thick. Allow to cool, and then transfer to a small serving bowl. Cover with plastic wrap and refrigerate.

Cold food needs more spice, so before serving, adjust the seasonings and add cayenne, if you like.

Meanwhile, cut the cheese into 1/2-inch slices.

In a small nonstick skillet over low heat, heat the oil and garlic until the garlic begins to turn golden, about 2 minutes. With a slotted spoon, remove the garlic and reserve. Add the cheese in one layer and fry until warm and soft, about 1 minute. Remove the skillet from the heat and add the sherry. Cover the skillet and return it to the heat for 2 to 3 minutes.

Serve right in the skillet or slide the warm cheese onto a serving platter and top with the reserved garlic. Present the tomato jam and bread on the side.

SERRANO HAM WITH DRUNKEN MELON
Serves 6 to 8

Wine and ham. Don Giovanni certainly knew what to serve his guests to entice them to distraction.

The sweet orange liqueur–accented melon nicely balances the slightly salty Serrano ham.

For a pretty presentation, serve the melon balls in the hollowed melon half. Refreshing, delicious, and gorgeous.

- 1 honeydew or cantaloupe melon
- 2 to 3 tablespoons Cointreau or other orange liqueur
- 1 scallion, thinly sliced
- 3 tablespoons minced fresh mint leaves
- Zest of 1 orange
- ½ pound Serrano ham, thinly sliced

Cut the melon in half and, using a melon baller or teaspoon, scoop out the flesh into a large bowl. Reserve one hollowed-out melon half to use later as a serving bowl.

Pour Cointreau over the melon balls and gently stir in the scallion, mint, and orange zest.

Cover the bowl with plastic wrap and refrigerate for at least 30 minutes and up to 4 hours so the flavors can mingle.

To serve, arrange the ham slices on a serving platter. Put the melon salad into the reserved melon half and serve alongside the ham.

Cioccolata, caffè, vini, prosciutti

Chocolate, coffe, wine, ham

Cerca divertir tutti . . .

Try to amuse everyone . . .

DON GIOVANNI

SPICY SCALLOP SEVICHE
Serves 6

The tiny bay scallops sparkle with specks of red, green, and yellow bell peppers in this cool yet spicy dish.

The citrus "cooks" the scallops fairly quickly, so assemble all your ingredients in the morning and toss them together just as guests arrive.

Warm foods taste spicier, so this cool dish may be a good time for fiery Scotch bonnet chile peppers. If you prefer less heat, go with the milder jalapeño.

- Freshly squeezed juice and zest of 1 lemon
- Freshly squeezed juice and zest of 1 lime
- 2 tablespoons dry sherry
- ½ Scotch bonnet pepper, or 1 jalapeño pepper, finely minced
- ¼ red bell pepper, finely minced
- ¼ green bell pepper, finely minced
- ¼ yellow bell pepper, finely minced
- 2 tablespoons finely minced Spanish onion
- 2 tablespoons extra-virgin olive oil
- ¾ pound bay scallops
- 3 tablespoons finely chopped cilantro
- 2 tablespoons finely chopped fresh mint
- Salt and freshly milled black pepper

In a bowl, combine the citrus juices, sherry, all the peppers, onion, and oil until well blended. Add the scallops, cilantro, and mint and gently stir to combine.

Season to taste with salt and pepper. Top with the citrus zest.

Serve immediately in a small bowl or on skewers.

WARM MARINATED OLIVES
Serves 6 to 8

Warm olives taste nothing at all like cold ones. It's as if they are a completely different food.

You'll be amazed at the extra levels of flavor that the garlic, onion, and honey provide. You can serve the olives immediately, but if possible, allow them to marinate at room temperature overnight. The olives really absorb the flavor that way. Just reheat them before serving. Outstanding.

½ Spanish onion, thinly sliced

3 tablespoons extra-virgin olive oil

4 cloves garlic, thinly sliced

2 tablespoons sherry vinegar

1 tablespoon honey

2 cups Spanish olives, about 9 ounces, drained and well rinsed

1 tablespoon pink peppercorns

2 tablespoons finely chopped fresh thyme, or 1 teaspoon dried

2 tablespoons fresh oregano leaves, or 1 teaspoon dried

In a medium skillet over medium-high heat, sauté the onion in oil until golden, about 5 minutes. Add the garlic, vinegar, and honey and sauté for about 30 seconds, until the vinegar evaporates. Add the olives and peppercorns, cover, and sauté until the olives are warmed through, about 2 minutes.

Serve topped with the thyme and oregano.

FIGARO'S FIERY SALMON SEVICHE
Serves 4 to 6

I have to confess something. Though I love seviche and always order it in restaurants, I only just recently started preparing it at home. I'm not entirely sure why I waited so long. Perhaps I was insecure about serving raw fish, or maybe I thought it was too complicated to make. Whatever my reluctance, I'm glad I got over it.

In truth, this dish is embarrassingly simple to prepare, even for novice seviche makers like me. It's just a matter of chopping a few ingredients and tossing them into a bowl. Elegant, with a wonderful range of flavors, from crunchy cool to fiery hot, this is a tapas must-try.

¾ pound salmon, minced

2 scallions, finely chopped

3 tablespoons finely chopped cilantro

2 tablespoons extra-virgin olive oil

2 teaspoons prepared Dijon mustard

Freshly squeezed juice and zest of 1 lime

½ Scotch bonnet pepper, very finely minced

Salt and freshly milled black pepper

Cucumber, peeled and sliced, optional

Vegetable chips, optional

Combine the salmon, scallions, cilantro, oil, mustard, juice and zest, and Scotch bonnet in a bowl. Season to taste with salt and pepper.

Serve immediately, accompanied by cucumber slices or vegetable chips if desired.

Pablo Elvira in *Il Barbiere di Siviglia*

CLAMS WITH SALSA VERDE
Serves 4 to 6

This tangy cilantro-lime salsa will tingle your palate in waves. First you'll be hit with the tantalizing aroma and zip of fresh cilantro, then the mild acidic goodness of lime, and finally the sharp but slightly sweet red onion and jalapeño combination.

This simple-to-assemble, no-cook sauce brings out the delicate brininess of clams but is terrific with all sorts of seafood. Try it on grilled fish too.

1 cup cilantro leaves

³/₄ cup fresh parsley leaves

¹/₄ cup chopped red onion

¹/₄ cup freshly squeezed lime juice

1 jalapeño pepper, roughly chopped

4 tablespoons extra-virgin olive oil

Salt and freshly milled black pepper

4 cloves garlic, thinly sliced

¹/₂ cup sweet sherry

2 dozen littleneck clams or cockles, in shells, well scrubbed

To prepare the salsa, puree the cilantro, parsley, onion, lime juice, jalapeño, and 2 tablespoons of the oil in a food processor until smooth. Season to taste with salt and pepper. Reserve.

Heat the remaining 2 tablespoons of oil in a large stockpot over medium heat. Add the garlic and cook about 1 minute, until soft. Remove the pot from the heat, add the sherry and clams, and cover. Return the pot to the heat and simmer the clams for about 6 minutes, or until the shells open.

Place the clams on a serving platter and top each with a dollop of salsa. Serve the remaining salsa on the side.

OPERA NOTE

After *La Bohème* and *Aida*, *Carmen* is the third most performed work in the Metropolitan Opera's repertoire. Since its first Met performance in 1884, *Carmen* has been staged not only in its original French but also in Italian and German. Georges Bizet never knew of *Carmen*'s success. He died at age thirty-six, just three months after its 1875 world premiere.

DON GIOVANNI'S OCTOPUS WITH POTATOES
Serves 4 to 6

Think you don't like octopus? You'll change your tune after tasting this dish. Octopus is nicely chewy, with a gorgeous color and a sublime flavor. It was even considered by Don Giovanni to be an aphrodisiac. Thanks to the many ready-made canned octopus options available in the Spanish foods section of most supermarkets, you now have an easy way to prepare one of the classic tapas—octopus with potatoes.

Of course, if you're already an octopus lover, prepare it from scratch. Just simmer ¾ pound of tentacles in gently boiling salted water until tender, about 30 minutes. Then slice the tentacles into bite-sized pieces and follow the directions below.

This dish can be made in advance and, in fact, tastes even better if it's eaten the next day.

- **2 to 3 red potatoes, about 1 pound, peeled and cut into 1½-inch cubes**
- **2 stalks celery with inner leaves, finely sliced**
- **½ red onion, finely chopped, about ½ cup**
- **¼ cup extra-virgin olive oil**
- **1 to 2 tablespoons sherry vinegar**
- **1 tablespoon capers, drained**
- **Freshly squeezed juice of 1 lemon**
- **Three 4-ounce cans octopus packed in olive oil, drained**
- **Salt and freshly milled black pepper**
- **Red pepper flakes or crushed chile peppers**
- **3 tablespoons minced fresh parsley**

In a large saucepan, bring a quart of salted water to a boil. Add the potatoes and cook until tender, about 10 minutes. Drain and place the potatoes in a large bowl. While they are still hot, toss with the celery, onion, oil, vinegar, capers, lemon juice, and octopus.

Season to taste with salt, black pepper, and red pepper flakes. Just before serving, top with parsley.

SAVORY PORK EMPANADAS
Serves 6 to 8

Empanada comes from the Spanish verb *empanar*, which means "to bake in pastry." Thanks to ready-made puff pastry sheets, it's a snap to *empanar*. The filling comes together in minutes and bakes up golden brown every time.

The ground pork, brown sugar, orange liqueur, and fennel seeds make a succulent, easy-to-prepare filling that's aromatic, moist, and flavorful.

6 ounces ground pork or beef

2 large eggs

3 ounces jarred piquillo peppers, or ½ red bell pepper, roasted and minced

¼ cup finely minced red onion

3 tablespoons Cointreau, or other orange liqueur

2 tablespoons dark brown sugar

1½ tablespoons fennel seeds

½ teaspoon cayenne

¼ teaspoon salt

1 box frozen puff pastry, thawed

Flour, for dusting

Combine the ground meat, 1 of the eggs, the peppers, onion, Cointreau, brown sugar, fennel, cayenne, and salt in a bowl and mix well.

Preheat the oven to 350°F. Beat the remaining egg in a small bowl.

Roll out the puff pastry ⅛ inch thick on a floured work surface. Using a 3-inch round cookie-cutter, press out about 16 dough circles. Place 1 tablespoon of the meat mixture on each circle, fold in half, and press the edges with the tip of a fork to seal.

Brush the top of each empanada with beaten egg and place on a lightly greased nonstick baking sheet. Bake for 20 minutes, or until golden brown. Serve warm.

Gerald Finley, baritone extraordinaire, carried the famed *Don Giovanni* sensuality to new heights in his interpretation of the role during the Met's 2004–2005 season. In the banquet scene he ate real pasta with gusto and even massaged it into his face and hair!

L'amour est un oiseau rebelle

Love is a rebellious bird

Que nul ne peut apprivoiser,

That nobody can tame,

Et c'est bien en vain qu'on l'appelle,

And it's useless to call him

S'il lui convient de refuser!

If he doesn't feel like answering you!

Rien n'y fait, menace ou prière,

Nothing is any use, threats or prayers,

L'un parle bien, l'autre se tait;

One speaks sweet words, another is silent;

Et c'est l'autre que je préfère,

And it is the other I prefer

Il n'a rien dit, mais il me plaît.

He says nothing, but I like him.

CARMEN

ROASTED PEPPER AND CHEESE EMPANADAS
Serves 6 to 8

Melty warm cheese, sweet piquillo peppers, mellow roasted garlic, and a hint of cayenne heat—these create a culinary counterpoint that smoothly melds to tingle your tongue with pleasure.

Don't worry if you can't find fresh piquillo peppers; the results are still outstanding if you substitute sweet red bell peppers. In a pinch you can even use jarred ready-roasted peppers.

1 box frozen puff pastry, thawed

Flour, for dusting

4 to 6 piquillo peppers, or 1 red bell pepper, roasted, peeled, seeded, and minced

¼ pound tetilla or manchego cheese, coarsely grated

6 to 7 cloves garlic, thinly sliced

Cayenne

1 large egg, beaten

Preheat the oven to 350°F.

Roll out the puff pastry ⅛ inch thick on a floured work surface. Using a 3-inch round cookie-cutter, press out about 16 dough circles.

Place about ½ tablespoon of the peppers, ½ tablespoon of the cheese, several garlic slices, and a sprinkle of cayenne on each circle, fold in half, and press the edges with the tip of a fork to seal.

Brush the tops of the empanadas with egg and place on a lightly greased nonstick baking sheet. Bake for 20 minutes, or until golden brown. Serve warm.

WARM DATES WITH SERRANO HAM AND ALMONDS
Serves 4 to 6

It's hard to believe that something this delicious uses just three ingredients and takes only minutes to make.

The dates seem to melt into the oven-crisped Serrano ham, giving them a jamlike sweetness. The almonds add just the perfect crunch.

12 Medjool dates

¼ cup sliced almonds

12 paper-thin slices Serrano ham

Preheat the oven to 350°F.

With a sharp knife, make a small cut lengthwise in the top of each date and remove the pit.

In a small, dry nonstick skillet over medium-low heat, lightly toast the almonds for less than 1 minute. Using a teaspoon, fill the dates with the almonds.

Wrap a slice of ham around each date and place it onto an ungreased nonstick cookie sheet.

Bake about 5 minutes, until the dates are warm. Serve immediately.

Caution: Earplugs are recommended when serving; the spontaneous applause evoked by this dish may cause temporary deafness.

Justino Díaz and Grace Bumbry in *Carmen*

OPERA NOTE

Though *Carmen* is set in Spain, interestingly
Bizet never visited that country.
He felt a visit there would only confuse him.

Sweets

ITALIAN COMPOSERS OF THE 1800S WOULD STRATEGICALLY PLACE *ARIA DI SORBETTO*—a sorbet aria—at a point in an opera. These songs were always sung by a secondary character and didn't advance the story. They allowed patrons time to leave their seats to purchase sorbet and ices without missing important plot development.

"*Sempre gridi*" (ever smiling), in Act II of *Il Barbiere di Siviglia*, is one such *aria di sorbetto*.

LIME CILANTRO GRANITA
Serves 6

The flecks of bright green cilantro dotting this luscious dessert are stunning. This elegant granita is simple to make and refreshingly tart. It will leave guests "ever smiling."

- 1 cup sugar
- 1 cup freshly squeezed lime juice
- 1 cup cilantro leaves
- Zest of 1 lemon
- Zest of 1 lime
- Tequila, optional

In a medium saucepan, bring the sugar and 1 cup water to a boil. Simmer for 5 minutes until the syrup thickens. Meanwhile, in a blender, puree the lime juice and cilantro until the cilantro is quite fine.

Remove the saucepan from the heat and allow to cool. Refrigerate for 30 minutes until chilled, then stir in the cilantro mixture.

Pour the mixture into a shallow glass or plastic container and put it into the freezer for at least 2 hours. Mash with a fork before serving until it is slushy. If it has frozen solid, you can allow it to thaw until you can mash it. Serve topped with the lemon and lime zest and a splash of tequila, if using.

ROSE TRUFFLES
Makes about 24 truffles

These rose-scented, creamy, easy-to-make truffles are in honor of the "Habanera aria," which usually ends with Carmen giving Don José a flower. Don José later affirms his love with the "Flower Song."

- 6 ounces bittersweet chocolate
- 2 egg yolks
- 3 tablespoons unsalted butter
- 2 tablespoons rose syrup, or 1 tablespoon rose water
- Sherry
- Candied rose petals or cocoa powder for dusting

In a double boiler or in a glass or stainless steel bowl set over a pan of boiling water, heat the chocolate until it melts. Still working over the boiling water, beat in the egg yolks. Remove from the heat and stir in the butter until well combined, then stir in the rose syrup and a splash of sherry.

If necessary, transfer the chocolate mixture to a bowl, cover it with plastic wrap, and refrigerate for at least 6 hours until firm.

Form the chocolate into olive-sized balls, rolling them in your palms. Dust with crushed candied rose petals or cocoa powder and arrange on a serving plate.

ALMOND CAKE ACCENTED WITH CITRUS
Serves 8 to 10

End your tapas party on a sweet note by offering guests a mouthful of Spanish sunshine.

Here is a classic Spanish recipe for a light, flourless always-moist cake bursting with the tang of lemon, lime, and orange zests.

Butter, for the pan

Flour, for the pan

8 ounces blanched almonds

Zest of 2 oranges

Zest of 1 lemon

Zest of 1 lime

6 extra-large eggs, separated

¾ cup granulated sugar

Pinch of salt

Confectioners' sugar, for serving

Almond slices, for serving

Preheat the oven to 450°F and place the rack in the center position. Generously butter a 10-inch springform pan and dust it with flour.

In a food processor, grind the almonds with half of the orange zest and all the lemon and lime zest until very fine. Add the egg yolks and granulated sugar and process until well combined. At this point the batter will be very thick and sticky.

In a separate bowl, using an electric mixer, beat the egg whites with a pinch or two of salt until stiff peaks form. Add the almond mixture, a little at a time, to the egg whites, mixing with each addition. Pour the mixture into the prepared pan.

Place the pan in the oven and turn the temperature down to 300°F. Bake for 30 to 35 minutes, or until a toothpick stuck in the center of the cake comes out clean. Allow to cool.

Sprinkle with confectioners' sugar, the remaining orange zest, and a scattering of almond slices.

CHOCOLATE "CHORIZO"
Serves 10 to 12 (three 6-inch "chorizos")

Kids love to help make this whimsical yet wonderful-tasting sweet because they get to crush cookies and pound nuts. The nuts and cookie bits are then stirred into melted chocolate and formed into a chorizo-shaped log. When you slice it, the log looks just like real chorizo sausage.

Flavor the chocolate with any combination of your favorite liqueurs, extracts, and spices. Try the recipe also with chocolate liqueur and cinnamon or Cointreau and a pinch of orange zest.

> 2 ounces bittersweet chocolate
>
> 4 tablespoons (½ stick) unsalted butter
>
> ½ cup superfine sugar
>
> 2 tablespoons Tia Maria or other coffee liqueur, or espresso coffee
>
> 1 tablespoon cocoa powder
>
> ½ cup coarsely crushed cookies such as biscotti or shortbread
>
> ¼ cup coarsely crushed hazelnuts

In a double boiler or in a glass or stainless steel bowl set over a pan of boiling water, melt the chocolate and butter. Once the chocolate has melted, mix in the sugar until dissolved. Add the Tia Maria and cocoa powder and stir until well combined. Stir in the cookies and nuts.

Divide the mixture into thirds. Transfer each third to a sturdy plastic bag and shape into a chorizo log about 6 inches long. Refrigerate until firm, about 2 hours.

To serve, cut a few slices of one "chorizo" and arrange with the remaining uncut piece on a small wooden cutting board or platter.

Don Giovanni

Ehi, Caffè!

Cioccolata!

Sorbetti!

Confetti!

DON GIOVANNI

Chapter Three

Il est temps qu'on se régale,

It is time to treat yourself

Ma cuisine est sans

My cuisine is without

égale!

equal!

MANON

Très Chic
Cocktail Party

JULES-ÉMILE-FRÉDÉRIC MASSENET'S OPERA *MANON*—the quintessential example of the late-nineteenth-century Parisian Belle Époque—begins with a meal at a hostelry. Berlioz's *Benvenuto Cellini* opens as Cellini and fellow workers drink a toast to their art, *"Honneur aux maîtres ciseleurs."* And *Les Contes d'Hoffmann* starts at a tavern with a song sung by the invisible spirits of wine and beer. The French love of food and drink is abundantly on display in their operas filled with dancing, masked balls, Mardi Gras, and bacchanals, and thus French composers provide a splendid excuse for a party.

A *Très Chic* Cocktail Party is a splendid way to celebrate these delightful composers and their works. Begin with a tasting of French wines and cheeses. Even if you're a wine novice, you will enjoy hosting a tasting: It's a great way to learn about wine and discover new kinds of cheeses. The festivities achieve Grand Opera heights of style with cocktails such as the refreshing Faust's Potion, served with an assortment of classic French nibbles like Pâté Manon with Chambord Glaze and Herbes de Provence Onion Tart. End with the stunning masterpiece of French desserts, Raspberry and Lavender Dacquoise, and send your guests home singing *en Français*.

Menu

COCKTAILS
French Kiss

Opera Cocktail

Eiffel Tower

French Martini

Faust's Potion

SAVORY NIBBLES
French Canapés

Warm Cheese Puffs

Pâté Manon with Chambord Glaze

Herbes de Provence Onion Tart

Tapenade Red Potato Bites

Les Troyens *Smoked Trout Custard*

SWEET NIBBLES
Pears Belle-Hélène

Chocolate Almond Macaroons

Raspberry and Lavender Dacquoise

PREVIOUS PAGES: *Manon*

Cocktails

A NIGHT AT THE OPERA IN THE NINETEENTH CENTURY was radically different from what we experience today. Audiences back then chatted, ate, and drank throughout the performance. They would even gamble during the show at tables set up by the management in the lobby or at the rear of the theater. Composers received a cut of the gambling profits!

The only reserved seats for the opera back then were the boxes, which seated four to six patrons. The orchestra seats were not numbered and were offered on a first-come, first-served basis. The wealthy would send their servants ahead to sit in choice seats until they arrived.

FRENCH WINE TASTING

Hosting a wine tasting is a delightful way to increase your wine knowledge.

There are a variety of ways to organize a tasting. For instance, you can focus on white wine and serve two or three varieties of Chardonnay, Sauvignon Blanc, and Pinot Gris. Or, you might concentrate on one grape variety, Chenin Blanc for example, and serve selections of wines made from it, such as Vouvray, Saumur, and Savennières.

Another option is to offer wines from a single region. For example, you might offer a variety of rosés from Provence or a sampling of reds from Bordeaux.

For a first-time wine tasting, I recommend offering a choice of four kinds of white and four reds. You will be able to get about ten two-ounce tasting-sized portions from each bottle. So plan on one bottle of each wine for eight to ten guests.

Set a place with a separate wineglass for each wine to be tasted for each guest. If you are offering a total of eight wines to eight guests you'll need sixty-four glasses. If you don't own that many glasses you may rent or, if you prefer, purchase inexpensive wineglasses. Another option is to give everyone a bowl of water and a large napkin and have the guest rinse the same glass between tastings.

If you plan to taste both reds and whites, be sure to set out two types of glasses. White wine is generally served in a smaller, narrower glass to help maintain the wine's cool temperature. Red wine is served in larger, more open glass that allows space for the wine's aroma and flavor to develop.

THERE ARE THREE STEPS IN EVALUATING A WINE:

ONE, hold the glass up to the light and observe the wine's color and clarity.

TWO, smell the wine. Hold the glass by the stem and gently swirl the wine to release its aromas. Put your nose down into the glass and inhale. Yes, stick your nose right into the glass. That's how the professionals do it!

Note the fragrances. Does the wine have a floral bouquet? The rosés of Provence smell of lavender, and red Bordeaux wines have the fragrance of violets.

Do you smell fruit? Chardonnay can have hints of apple, and Pinot Noir can evoke black cherries, while Chablis is often compared to a peach orchard.

THREE, take a small sip. Hold it in your mouth and inhale deeply. What flavors do you experience? Are there hints of fruit? Many young reds taste of berries. What other flavors do you taste? Chardonnay has a hint of sweet butter flavor, and Merlot has hints of herbs.

There are many lush terms used for the smells and tastes of wines. They have been described as fresh, earthy, as tasting of velvet or honey, and as smelling like a wonderful cigar box, newly cut oak, or clean minerals.

Mirella Freni in *Roméo et Juliette*

L'heure s'envole

The hour flies past

Joyeuse et folle,

in wild merriment.

Au passage il faut la saisir!

We must seize it as it goes by!

Cueillons les roses

Let us gather the roses

Pour nous écloses

that have bloomed for us

Dans la joie et dans le plaisir.

in joy and delight.

ROMÉO ET JULIETTE

FRENCH KISS
Serves 1

1 ounce Courvoisier V.S.

$1/2$ ounce sweetened lemon juice

4 ounces champagne

Lemon peel, for garnish

Pour the Courvoisier and lemon juice into a wineglass. Top with champagne. Twist the lemon peel over the drink and drop it into the glass.

OPERA COCKTAIL
Serves 1

This classic opera-lover's cocktail is wonderfully sweet and refreshing.

$1 1/2$ ounces gin

$3/4$ ounce Dubonnet rouge

$1/2$ ounce maraschino liqueur or Chambord

Orange peel, for garnish

Combine the gin, Dubonnet, and liqueur in a shaker with crushed ice and mix well. Pour into a chilled cocktail glass. Twist the orange peel over the drink and drop it into the glass.

OPERA NOTE

Roméo et Juliette (December 14, 1891) was the first French-language performance at the Metropolitan Opera House. *Faust* had been performed there earlier but in Italian or German—and on one occasion in both languages, when Julius Perotti substituted for an ill Max Alvary on December 26, 1888, and sang the title role in Italian against the German of the rest of the cast.

EIFFEL TOWER
Serves 1

1 ounce vodka

1 ounce cognac

½ ounce anisette

½ ounce Triple Sec

Combine the vodka, cognac, anisette, and Triple Sec in a shaker with crushed ice and mix well. Strain into a tall cocktail glass filled with ice cubes.

FRENCH MARTINI
Serves 1

2 ounces pineapple juice

1 ounce vodka

½ ounce Chambord

Pineapple wedge, for garnish

Combine the pineapple juice, vodka, and Chambord in a shaker with crushed ice and mix well. Strain into a martini glass and garnish with a pineapple wedge.

FAUST'S POTION
Serves 1

A light and refreshing classic French punch.

3 ounces red wine, preferably Bordeaux

1 ounce cognac or brandy

Sparkling water

1 tablespoon strawberry sorbet

1 whole strawberry, for garnish

Pour the wine and cognac into a wine glass. Top with a splash of sparkling water and the sorbet. Garnish the glass with a strawberry.

Vin ou bière,

Wine or beer,

Bière ou vin,

Beer or wine,

Que mon verre

As long as my glass

Soit plein!

Is full!

Sans vergogne,

Without shame,

Coup sur coup,

One after the other,

Un ivrogne

A drunkard

Boit tout!

Drinks everything!

FAUST

Savory Nibbles

FRENCH CHEESE TASTING

Just as with a wine tasting, it is best to offer only six to eight cheeses for a tasting. Label each cheese so guests can remember which they liked best. I use folded place cards as labels. Also number the cheeses in the order to be tried. Begin with mild, progress to medium-flavored, and end with sharp cheeses.

There are hundreds of French cheeses, so you can organize a tasting in many ways. You might try an assortment of soft cheeses; or you can focus on goat's-milk cheeses; or you might feature a particular region of France, like Franche-Comté, near the Alps.

Here is a suggested list of my favorite cheeses.

Mild cheeses

CHAOURCE—fruity, ivory-colored cow's-milk cheese with a white rind and that pairs very well with white wine.

FOURME D'AMBERT—cow's-milk blue cheese with a yellowish rind and an unbelievable earthy, nutty flavor.

SELLES-SUR-CHER—goat's-milk cheese with a light nutty flavor. The gray rind may be eaten.

TOME DES BAUGES OR TOME DE SAVOIE—both have a lovely, delicate flavor and are great snacking cheeses.

VALENÇAY—goat's-milk cheese with a nutty flavor.

Medium cheeses

BANON—attractively leaf-wrapped goat's-milk cheese with a nutty flavor. It's a favorite in Provence and comes with a variety of seasonings, including herb and black pepper.

COMTÉ—aromatic cow's-milk cheese that has a fruity flavor if it was produced in the summer and a lovely nut flavor if it was made in the winter.

CLOCKWISE FROM TOP: **Pouligny Saint-Pierre (pyramid), Banon (wrapped in a leaf), Mimolette, Brie, Morbier (with a line of plant coal in the middle), Petite Basque, Bleu de Gex, Warm Cheese Puffs (on plate to the left)**

MORBIER—from France's acclaimed Franche-Comté region, aromatic cow's-milk cheese with a hint of fruit taste. A slice looks a little like a layer cake with a center of dark frosting. The "frosting" is actually plant coal, which adds a subtle smoky and earthy overtone.

POULIGNY SAINT-PIERRE—fine goat's-milk cheese with a nutty citrus taste. Its Eiffel tower shape makes it an attractive addition to any cheese platter.

SAINT-NECTAIRE—cow's-milk cheese with an earthy flavor that has the fragrance of a field of hay after a spring shower and the hint of a taste of nuts and spices.

Strong cheeses

LANGRES—soft cow's-milk cheese with a rind that smells a little like a damp forest. Warning! This slightly salty, strongly flavored cheese is not for the cheese novice.

LIVAROT—soft cow's-milk cheese, popular in Normandy, with an aroma of fine herbs and taste of citrus.

MAROILLES—strongly flavored cow's-milk cheese.

ROQUEFORT—ewe's-milk blue cheese ripened in natural stone cellars. The French call this tangy, pleasingly salty-tasting blue the "king of cheeses."

PAIRING CHEESE AND WINE

If you want to serve French wines with your French cheese tasting, here are some tried-and-true pairings. Mild cheeses pair nicely with the spicy, slightly sweet Chenin Blanc wines; medium cheeses with Merlot and Pinot Noir; and strong cheeses with Cabernet Sauvignon. Goat's-milk cheese is delicious with Sauvignon Blanc. One of the all-time classic cheese-wine pairings is Roquefort and Sauternes.

Remember, there are no cheese police and no one will issue a summons if you violate these suggestions. The fun of a cheese and wine tasting is to taste lots of cheeses and wines in lots of combinations and come to your own conclusions.

Garnishes

ONE OF THE JOYS OF STROLLING DOWN A BOULEVARD IN PARIS is peeking into the windows of food shops to see all the artistic garnishes the French invent—sculpted flowers created from bits of carrot and herbs fixed in savory aspics, candied whole fruits, carved vegetables and fruits that look like animals or flowers.

If you like to play with your food, a *Très Chic* Cocktail Party is the perfect excuse to experiment with classic French garnishes. Here are three of my favorite garnishes that add a *très jolie* touch and don't require an artist's skills to create.

KUMQUAT BASKETS
Makes 6 baskets

Guests can just pop the whole raspberry-filled kumquat basket into their mouths. A deliciously refreshing garnish.

6 fresh kumquats
6 fresh raspberries
6 tiny fresh mint leaves

With a sharp knife, cut 2 equal-sized wedges out of the top half of each kumquat, leaving a tiny center section intact for the basket's handle. Using a grapefruit spoon or chopstick, scoop out the kumquat flesh, taking care not to tear the "handle."

Fill each basket with a raspberry and a mint leaf.

J'aurai grand soin

I shall regale

De me soûler, non d'allégresse,

My pressing needs, not with romancing,

Mais de la vraie et bonne ivresse!

But with good and downright
heavy drinking!

DON QUIXOTE

TOMATO ROSES
Makes 3 roses

3 very firm medium-sized tomatoes
Mint leaves

Starting at the bottom, peel the skin from each tomato in one long, thin spiral strip. Use a sharp knife and don't try for fine edges. A ragged edge makes the rose look more realistic. Reserve the flesh of the tomato for another use.

Roll up the skin into a rose shape. Decorate the rose with mint leaves.

RADISH CHRYSANTHEMUMS
Makes 3 chrysanthemums

3 small radishes

Hold the radish by the stem section and, using a sharp knife, make as many deep, vertical cuts as you can. Turn the radish 90 degrees and repeat.

Put the cut radishes into a bowl of ice water until ready to serve. The ice water will cause the radishes to open into a chrysanthemum shape.

OPERA NOTE

On October 22, 1883, for its gala opening, the Metropolitan Opera House performed *Faust*. Christine Nilsson, who set an international standard in the role of Marguerite, sang at this performance and encored the "Jewel Song." She was so prized an interpreter of the role that when she performed it in St. Petersburg and opened her onstage jewelry box, she found real jewels, courtesy of the Russian royal family.

Faust was also performed on November 27, 1893, when the Met first introduced electric lights to its audience. The most highly prized, magically lit seats in the lower ring of boxes were later nicknamed the "Diamond Horseshoe."

As Edith Wharton correctly notes in *The Age of Innocence, Faust* was performed at the Met every season through the early 1900s.

The opera is even popular with comic strip characters. Bianca Castafiore, a flamboyant opera singer in the *Tintin* series, is often heard singing Marguerite's "Jewel Song." Her favorite line is, *Ah! je ris de me voir si belle en ce miroir!* (*Ah! I laugh to see how lovely I look in this mirror!*), which she repeats often and loudly.

Nicolai Ghiaurov in *Faust*

FRENCH CANAPÉS
Serves 6

Canapé—what a wonderfully retro word! It means "couch" in French and just about any savory can sit on these miniature open-faced sandwiches—paté, caviar, cheese, and cold cuts of all sorts. The key to canapés, whether cut into triangles, squares, or circles, is to be sure they are very thin and easy to eat. It should be one or two bites at most.

Here are three of my favorites—the prototypical French ham with sweet butter accented with a hint of Dijon and cornichon; a classic watercress updated with a touch of smoky sweet paprika; and a very pretty shrimp canapé with aioli.

FOR 12 HAM CANAPÉS
3 thin slices white bread

2 tablespoons butter, softened

3 thin slices smoked ham

Dijon or honey mustard

3 cornichons, thinly sliced

Butter the bread and top each slice with ham. Using a very sharp knife, cut off the crusts. Cut the sandwiches in half diagonally to create 2 triangles and then in half again diagonally, creating a total of 4 triangles per slice. Top each triangle with a tiny dollop of mustard and a cornichon slice.

FOR 6 WATERCRESS CANAPÉS
6 thin slices black bread

3 tablespoons butter, softened

¼ teaspoon sweet smoked paprika, plus more for garnish

1 hard-boiled egg, minced

Salt and freshly milled black pepper

6 sprigs watercress

Using a 2½-inch round cookie-cutter, cut out circles from the center of the black bread. Mix the butter, paprika, and egg in a small bowl until very well combined. Season to taste with salt and pepper.

Spread the butter-egg mixture onto the bread circles and gently press watercress leaves into the center of each circle. Garnish with a sprinkle of paprika.

FOR 12 AIOLI SHRIMP CANAPÉS
2 tablespoons mayonnaise

1 clove garlic, finely mashed

2 teaspoons freshly squeezed lemon juice

½ teaspoon olive oil

Salt and freshly milled black pepper

3 thin slices white bread

6 small shrimp, poached and thinly sliced or chopped

Zest of ½ lemon

To make the aioli, combine the mayonnaise, garlic, lemon juice, and olive oil in a small bowl until well mixed. Season to taste with salt and pepper.

Spread the aioli onto each slice of bread. Using a very sharp knife, cut off the crusts from the bread. Cut the sandwiches in half to create 2 rectangles and then in half again, creating a total of 4 squares per slice.

Top each section with shrimp and a bit of lemon zest.

"Ah, music!
What a beautiful art!
But what a wretched
profession!"

GEORGES BIZET

WARM CHEESE PUFFS
Serves 8

These cheese puffs are mouthfuls of warm bliss.

Gougères in French, these delicious nibbles are made from cream puff dough, *pâte à choux*. If you've never made them, you are in for a real treat. Despite the intimidating name, this dough is simple to make.

You'll absolutely love having *pâte à choux* in your arsenal of recipes because once you learn the basic technique you'll be able to change it in dozens of ways, using all sorts of ingredients. You can add almost any spices and herbs, like cayenne, smoked paprika, or *herbes de Provence*, to a wide range of cheeses for simple variations to this basic recipe. You can even substitute seafood, bacon, or ham for the cheese. Best of all, you can also make sweets like cream puffs, profiteroles, and éclairs with it.

> **5 tablespoons unsalted butter, plus additional for the baking sheet**
>
> **1 cup whole milk**
>
> **1/2 teaspoon salt**
>
> **1 cup all-purpose flour**
>
> **5 large eggs**
>
> **1 1/2 cups grated cheese such as Comté, Beaufort, Gruyère, or Emmental (or 3/4 cup crumbled, if using a stronger cheese such as blue or Gorgonzola)**
>
> **1 teaspoon honey mustard**
>
> **Pinch of freshly milled black pepper**

Generously butter a large baking sheet. Preheat the oven to 375°F.

Combine the butter, milk, and salt in a medium saucepan over medium heat and bring just to a boil, then reduce the heat to low and cook until the butter is melted.

Remove from the heat and immediately add the flour, stirring with a wooden spoon until well combined. Return the saucepan to the stove and, over low heat, stir the mixture for about 1 minute, until the dough dries a little.

Remove the pan from the heat and blend in 4 of the eggs one at a time, stirring briskly with a wooden spoon until a smooth paste forms. Be sure that each egg is well incorporated before adding the next. The dough will look like paste at this point. Stir in the cheese, mustard, and pepper.

Beat the remaining egg in a small bowl.

Place tablespoon-sized portions of the dough onto the prepared baking sheet and, using a pastry brush, coat with the beaten egg. Bake for about 30 minutes, or until puffed and golden.

Natalie Dessay and Ramón Vargas in *Roméo et Juliette*

PÂTÉ MANON WITH CHAMBORD GLAZE
Serves 8

Pâté with the accent on the *e* is French for "pie." Without the accent it means "dough" or "paste."

Now, with the French lesson out of the way, let's discuss why, when there are so many ready-made versions, you should make your own pâté.

There are two reasons. One, it's delicious. Two, it's fun, partly because it's so easy to do. Just a quick sauté and a spin in the food processor and—voilà—you have pâté! But the real fun comes from decorating the top of the pâté. I use dried apricots and cherries to create my own culinary Monet or Seurat. Sometimes I just make Van Gogh-esque sunflowers with strips of apricots. The Chambord gelatin is delicious and really shimmers, creating *un objet d'art* that the innkeeper in *Manon* would have been honored to serve.

1 large red onion, minced

5 tablespoons unsalted butter

1 pound chicken livers

2 dried apricots, finely minced, plus more
   for garnish

1 tablespoon dried cherries or cranberries, minced,
   plus more for garnish

1/4 teaspoon dried thyme

1/8 teaspoon ground allspice

3/4 cup Chambord or other black raspberry liqueur

1/3 cup heavy cream, plus more as needed

Salt and freshly milled black pepper

1 teaspoon powdered unflavored gelatin

1 baguette

2 tablespoons extra-virgin olive oil

In a medium skillet, sauté the onion in 3 tablespoons of the butter over medium heat for about 15 minutes, until the onion is golden. Add the livers, apricots, cherries, thyme, and allspice and cook for about 3 minutes. The liver should be pink in the center. Add 1/2 cup of the Chambord and cook for about 1 minute until the liqueur is absorbed. Remove from the heat and cover until cool.

Place the livers, the remaining 2 tablespoons of butter, and the cream into a food processor and purée. Add more cream if needed until the pâté is smooth. Season to taste with salt and pepper.

Place the pâté in a shallow serving container roughly 9 by 7 inches and top with a scattering of the reserved apricots and cherries. Set aside.

Place the gelatin in a small bowl and stir in 1/4 cup boiling water until the gelatin is dissolved. Add the remaining 1/4 cup Chambord and stir. Carefully pour the gelatin over the pate and refrigerate for 1 hour, or until set.

Just before serving, preheat the broiler and slice the baguette. Place the bread slices on a baking sheet and brush with olive oil. Toast each side of the bread under the broiler until light golden brown.

Present the pâté on a serving platter, surrounded with the warm baguette toasts.

Un pâté!

Non pas, messieurs

Un objet d'art!

MANON

Renée Fleming and company in *Manon*

HERBES DE PROVENCE
ONION TART
Serves 8

Onion tart, a sort of French pizza, is one of my favorite party nibbles. The topping combines sweet caramelized onions, rich oil-cured olives, and a hint of anchovy. The dough is flecked with *herbes de Provence*, which is a sublime blend of lavender, thyme, rosemary, and other aromatics.

> 1 package active dry yeast, about ¼ ounce
>
> 3 tablespoons extra-virgin olive oil, plus more as needed
>
> 2 tablespoons dried herbes de Provence
>
> ¾ teaspoon salt, plus more as needed
>
> 2 cups all-purpose flour
>
> 1 large red onion, thinly sliced
>
> 2 large Vidalia onions, thinly sliced
>
> 4 tablespoons (½ stick) unsalted butter
>
> Freshly milled black pepper
>
> 15 to 20 pitted oil-cured olives, chopped
>
> 3 to 4 anchovy fillets, minced

Combine ⅔ cup warm water with the yeast in a large bowl and let rest for 5 minutes. Stir in the oil, 1 tablespoon of the herbs, and the salt. Slowly add the flour, mixing until combined. Knead for 2 to 3 minutes, or until the dough is smooth.

Place the dough in a lightly oiled bowl, cover with a towel, and allow to rise in a warm place for about 1 hour.

Meanwhile, prepare the onion topping. Sauté the onions and remaining tablespoon of herbs in the butter in a medium skillet over medium heat for about 20 minutes, or until very soft. Season to taste with salt and pepper.

Preheat the oven to 425°F. Generously oil a 9-by-13-inch baking pan and reserve.

Put the dough onto the prepared baking pan and, pressing down with your hands, push it to the edges. Spread the onion mixture over the dough. Top with a scattering of olives and anchovies. Drizzle with olive oil.

Bake for 30 minutes, or until the crust is golden.

Slice the tart into individual-serving-sized sections.

TAPENADE RED POTATO BITES
Serves 8

Tapenade is a no-cook, easy-to-assemble scrumptious appetizer of olives and seasonings. It takes just a few seconds in a food processor to achieve instant gratification. You'll forever banish ready-made tapenade from your pantry.

The tapenade is nestled into tiny potatoes for a beautiful and delectable presentation. You'll especially like the creamy simplicity of potatoes, which balance the salty earthiness of the olive mixture.

- 8 small red new potatoes
- 3/4 cup pitted oil-cured black olives
- 1/2 cup assorted minced fresh herbs such as basil, rosemary, and parsley, plus more for garnish
- 2 to 3 cloves garlic
- 1 tablespoons capers, drained
- 2 ounces tuna packed in olive oil, drained, or 2 anchovy fillets
- 1/4 cup extra-virgin olive oil
- Freshly squeezed juice and zest of 1/2 lemon, plus more if desired
- Freshly milled black pepper

Boil the potatoes until just tender, about 12 minutes. Reserve.

In a food processor, combine the olives, herbs, garlic, capers, and tuna and puree until combined. Add the oil and lemon juice to taste and puree until smooth. Season to taste with pepper.

To serve, cut the potatoes in half and, using a melon baller, scoop out the center to create a hollow. Fill the hollow with a dollop of tapenade and arrange on a serving platter. Garnish with the lemon zest and a sprinkle of minced herbs.

LES TROYENS SMOKED TROUT CUSTARD
Serves 6

You'll love how pretty this dish looks. The dill rises as it bakes and creates a lovely top for this creamy, flavor-packed pâté-like custard. This is a particularly fitting dish for Berlioz's *Les Troyens*, as it is based on an authentic ancient Roman recipe from the world's oldest surviving cookbook, by Apicius. Despite its ancient roots, it's a light and modern hors d'oeuvre that might have been enjoyed by Dido and Aeneas.

- 1/2 cup heavy cream
- 1/2 cup whole milk
- 2 large egg yolks
- 1 large egg
- Freshly squeezed juice of 1 lemon
- 2 tablespoons chopped fresh dill, plus fronds for garnish
- 1/4 teaspoon salt
- 1/4 teaspoon freshly milled black pepper
- Pinch of ground allspice
- 4 ounces smoked trout, finely flaked
- 1/4 teaspoon capers, drained
- 2 to 3 shallots, minced
- 1 lemon, cut into wedges
- 1 French baguette, sliced

Preheat the oven to 400°F and place a rack in the center position. Put one 2-cup ramekin into a deep baking pan and set aside.

Whisk together the cream, milk, yolks, egg, lemon juice, dill, salt, pepper, and allspice until well incorporated. Stir in the trout.

Pour the custard into the ramekin. Fill the baking pan with hot water until it reaches three-fourths of the way up the ramekin. Cover the pan with aluminum foil.

Bake the custard until set and firm, about 50 minutes. Leave it in the oven, with the heat turned off, for an additional 10 to 15 minutes. It will set further as it cools.

To serve, put the ramekin onto a platter garnished with dill fronds. Serve with capers, minced shallots, lemon wedges, and sliced baguette.

Sweet Nibbles

FRENCH CHEFS HAVE A LONG TRADITION OF creating special dishes for operas and opera stars.

Auguste Escoffier, one of France's premier chefs of the late nineteenth century, invented many enduring recipes. One such recipe was Peach Melba, poached peaches topped with raspberry sauce and vanilla ice cream, which he created in 1892 for the beloved Australian diva Nellie Melba. He also invented thin "Melba" toasts in her honor.

The now-famous Opera Cake was introduced in Paris at the Exposition Culinaire of 1903 by Louis Clichy and then updated and reintroduced in the 1960s by the famed pastry chef Gaston Lenôtre.

The tradition continues today with Daniel Boulud, New York City's award-winning French chef, who created La Diva Renée au Chocolat for the lovely Renée Fleming.

PEARS BELLE-HÉLÈNE
Serves 6

In the late 1860s, several French chefs created dishes in honor of Offenbach's popular opera bouffe, *La belle Hélène*. The most enduring is Pears Belle-Hélène, a poached pear topped with pear brandy–spiked chocolate sauce and served with vanilla ice cream.

1 cup sugar

1 whole vanilla bean, split

6 very small pears, such as forelle

¼ cup heavy cream

4 ounces bittersweet chocolate, finely chopped

3 tablespoons unsalted butter

2 to 3 tablespoons pear brandy such as Poire William

Vanilla ice cream

In a medium saucepan, combine 3 cups water with the sugar and vanilla bean and bring the mixture to a boil over high heat.

Peel and carefully core the pears, taking care to leave the stems intact. Add the pears to the boiling liquid. Reduce the heat to low, cover, and simmer for about 15 minutes, until the pears are tender but still firm. Leave the pears in the poaching liquid until you are ready to serve.

To make the chocolate sauce, warm the cream in a small saucepan over low heat. While still on low heat, add the chocolate and butter and stir until creamy. Remove from heat, stir in the pear brandy, and let cool to room temperature. Reserve, covered, until ready to use.

To serve, place a pear and a scoop of vanilla ice cream in a martini glass. Drizzle with the chocolate sauce.

OPERA NOTE

Giacomo Meyerbeer, who changed his name from Yaakov Liebmann Beer, was born in 1791 near Berlin but is remembered as the force behind French grand opera in mid-nineteenth-century Paris.

Meyerbeer, like his contemporary Rossini, prided himself on his cooking skills and appreciation of food. He was known to work for days with his housekeeper Maria Scotelli, making Italian biscotti, which he gave as Hanukkah gifts.

CHOCOLATE ALMOND MACAROONS
Makes 20 macaroons

Chewy, delicious, and oh-so-easy to make. These maca-roons with a hint of almond and drizzle of bittersweet chocolate are sublime. If you like, instead of topping the macaroons with chocolate you can insert a dark chocolate Hershey's Kiss inside each one before baking it. You get a gooey, warm center that's a divine alternative.

Macaroons might very well have been served at Éléazar's fifteenth-century Passover table, as versions have existed since the Middle Ages.

- **2 egg whites**
- **2 cups unsweetened coconut flakes**
- **1 teaspoon Amaretto or almond extract**
- **1 cup confectioners' sugar**
- **2 ounces semisweet chocolate**

Preheat oven to 350°F.

In a bowl, beat the egg whites with an electric mixer until stiff peaks form. Stir in the coconut and liqueur and mix until well combined. Slowly stir in the confectioners' sugar. Shape the mixture into walnut-sized balls and place them on a nonstick or parchment-lined cookie sheet about 1 inch apart.

Bake for 13 to 15 minutes, or until golden brown on the outside. Let cool.

Meanwhile, melt the chocolate in a double boiler (or a glass or stainless steel bowl set over a pan of boiling water) or in the microwave. Using a fork, drizzle the chocolate over the macaroons in a delicate crisscross pattern.

In preparing for a run of *Manon* at the Met in 2006, Ms. Fleming shared with *Opera News* magazine her two weaknesses: "Massenet and chocolate—and they go well together."

OPERA NOTE

Several French composers created operas inspired by Jewish themes and Old Testament stories, including *La Juive* (1835) by Fromental Halévy, *Hérodiade* (1881) by Jules Massenet, *Joseph* (1807) by Etienne Méhul, and *Samson et Dalila* (1877) by Camille Saint-Saëns.

Of course, other composers, notably Rossini (*Mosè in Egitto*, 1818), Verdi (*Nabucco*, 1842), and Richard Strauss (*Salome*, 1905), took biblical inspiration as well.

RASPBERRY AND LAVENDER DACQUOISE
Serves 10

The cloudlike layers of meringue are moist, thanks to a hint of chewy coconut. The fantastic fillings—sweet custard, juicy raspberries, and fluffy lavender-scented whipped cream—add both remarkable flavor and delicate aroma.

Complicated looking but actually easy to make, this is an impressive dessert that you'll serve again and again. I've perfected a foolproof recipe for the meringue layers. The custard and whipped cream nicely cover up any little cracks or mishaps, so do try this irresistible recipe.

You can vary the fruit and the flavorings of the whipped cream using other types of flower syrups, or even liqueurs.

    8 large eggs, separated

    ¼ teaspoon salt

    1 teaspoon cream of tartar

    1 cup superfine sugar

    3 teaspoons vanilla extract

    1 cup coconut flakes

    2 cups half-and-half

    ½ cup granulated sugar

    ½ cup all-purpose flour

    2 cups heavy cream

    ¼ cup lavender syrup

    2½ pints fresh raspberries

    Fresh mint leaves, for garnish

    Fresh lavender sprigs, optional, for garnish

To prepare the meringue, line two large cookie sheets with parchment. Using a pencil, outline four 8-inch circles onto the parchment.

Preheat the oven to 250°F.

In a large bowl, using an electric mixer, whip the egg whites, salt, and cream of tartar until stiff peaks form. If possible, use a standing mixer. Beat in ½ cup of the superfine sugar and 2 teaspoons of the vanilla until stiff. Beat in the remaining ½ cup superfine sugar. The egg whites should be shiny and stiff. Spread ¼ of the mixture on one of the outlined circles. This will be the top layer of the dacquoise, as it will bake higher than the coconut layers.

Fold the coconut into the remaining egg whites and then divide the mixture between the three remaining outlined circles. Those three will turn out flatter than the top layer.

Bake for about 1 hour on the center rack. Turn off the heat and let rest in the oven for another hour. Transfer the meringues while still on the parchment to a wire rack and allow to cool completely before removing them from the parchment paper. Store in an airtight container until ready to assemble.

To make the custard, bring the half-and-half just to a boil in a large saucepan over medium heat, then turn off the heat. Reserve.

Meanwhile, in a large bowl using an electric mixer, whip the egg yolks, granulated sugar, and remaining teaspoon of vanilla for about 4 minutes. When you lift the mixer blade, the mixture should form a thick ribbon. Slowly mix in the flour until well combined. Add 1 cup of the hot half-and-half to the bowl and mix well.

Turn the heat to medium again under the pan of half-and-half. Slowly, mixing constantly, pour the yolk mixture into the saucepan. Bring just to a boil, stirring the entire time. Reduce the heat to low and simmer for about 3 minutes, stirring constantly. Allow to cool. Pour into a bowl, cover with plastic wrap, and refrigerate until ready to use.

A few hours before serving, in a very large bowl using an electric mixer, whip the heavy cream until soft peaks form. Fold the lavender syrup into the whipped cream.

To assemble the dacquoise, place one of the coconut meringue layers on a serving plate. Spread half of the custard over the meringue. Top with 1 pint of the raspberries and then the second coconut meringue layer. Spread the meringue layer evenly with the whipped lavender cream and top with a third coconut meringue layer. Spread that layer evenly with remaining custard and top with another pint of raspberries and the fourth noncoconut meringue circle.

Before serving, top with lavender whipped cream, the remaining ½ pint of raspberries, mint leaves, and, if desired, fresh lavender. Cut with a serrated knife.

Chapter Four

Ein Grand Souper

Nur wer der Minne Macht entsagt,

Only he who forswears love's power,

Nur wer der Liebe Lust verjagt,

Only he who forfeits love's delight,

Nur der erzielt sich den Zauber,

Only he can attain the magic

zum Reif zu zwingen das Gold.

To fashion the gold into a ring.

DAS RHEINGOLD

GERMAN-LANGUAGE OPERA REMINDS ME OF lush, formal dinner parties filled with rich delicacies to be savored slowly in multiple courses over a long and luxurious evening. I entitled this chapter *Ein Grand Souper*, a grand supper, after lines in the delightful comic operetta *Die Fledermaus*, which invite guests to a feast of choice delicacies. There are so many wonderful dining scenes in German-language opera, like the lively supper scene in Act III of *Der Rosenkavalier* and the magical cooking moment in *Die Frau ohne Schatten*. One of my favorite scenes occurs in the prologue to *Ariadne auf Naxos*, which revolves around planning the entertainments for that evening's banquet.

Begin your feast of honoring German-language opera with a Charcuterie Platter with Three Homemade Mustards, the perfect partner for a hearty beer. The first course is a wildly delicious German Sour Cherry Soup, to be followed by either a fish or game dish—or both! As a finale, a light-as-a-song Flourless Apricot Poppy Seed Cake and Isolde's Marzipan Kisses, tiny almond treats, will bring a memorable evening to a close. *Guten Appetit!*

Menu

COCKTAIL
Salome Cocktail

APPETIZER
Charcuterie Platter with Three Homemade Mustards

FIRST COURSE
German Sour Cherry Soup

SECOND COURSE
Trout with Roasted Meyer Lemons
White Asparagus with Strawberry Champagne Vinaigrette

MAIN COURSE
Der Freischütz Venison Stew with Two Wines
Spaetzle with Spinach Nutmeg Butter
Freia's Golden Apples with Kale

DESSERT
Flourless Apricot Poppy Seed Cake
Isolde's Marzipan Kisses

Cocktail

RICHARD STRAUSS'S MOTHER was a member of the Pschorr family, owners of one of the oldest breweries in Germany, the renowned Hacker-Pschorr. The Munich-based company was famous for its adherence to the early-sixteenth-century Reinheitsgebot purity law, which mandated that beer be made with only four ingredients—malted barley, hops, yeast, and water.

Germany has a long beer tradition and today is home to well over a thousand breweries. Löwenbräu can trace its start to 1324, Augustinerbräu was begun by clergymen in 1328, and Hacker-Pschorr started business in 1417. Hofbräuhaus was founded by Duke Wilhelm V and, in a nod to its 1589 royal roots, still keeps a crown in the company's logo.

Serve an assortment of German beers before and during dinner. Besides a variety of beers and ales, try a sampling of German wheat beers such as Arcobräu Urweisse, Franziskaner, or Schöfferhoffer.

SALOME COCKTAIL
Serves 1

A bartender's classic, the Salome was first conceived in the 1920s at the start of the mixed-drink era. John the Baptist's head on a plate is represented in the drink's garnish, a maraschino cherry resting on a round slice of banana.

- **½ ounce sweet vermouth**
- **½ ounce Dubonnet**
- **½ ounce gin**
- **1 maraschino cherry, for garnish**
- **1 banana slice, for garnish**

Pour the vermouth, Dubonnet, and gin over ice into a short cocktail glass. Garnish with a toothpick-speared maraschino cherry on top of a slice of banana.

OPERA NOTE

The Metropolitan Opera House's American premiere of *Salome* (January 22, 1907) so shocked the audience with its subject matter and risqué veil dance that it received virtually no applause. J. Pierpont Morgan's scandalized daughter spearheaded a public outcry against *Salome*'s perceived immorality. The Met was forced to accede to public demand and cancel the three remaining scheduled performances.

Appetizer

SAUSAGES AND MUSTARD, LIKE STRAUSS AND VON HOFMANNSTHAL, were made for each other, and it is well worth a trip to a German specialty grocer to sample the wide variety available. You'll be amazed at the gorgeous array of cold cuts. They look like works of art, and they are all delicious. Select a variety for a charcuterie platter that's perfect with beer.

There are myriad kinds of German sausages and cold cuts. Here is a brief description of some of the goodies you can find in a German grocery shop:

BAUERNWURST—sausages seasoned with marjoram and mustard seeds.

BIERWURST—in German *bierwurst* means a sausage to eat with beer. These garlic-seasoned, deep red sausages are my favorite.

BOCKWURST OR WEISSWURST—mildly spiced sausages made with a mix of pork and veal.

BRÄGENWURST—long, thin smoked sausage made of pork brain, oatmeal, and onions.

BRATWURST—grainy, hearty pork sausage.

CERVELAT—dry cured beef or pork salami seasoned with garlic and herbs.

GELBWURST—light-colored, delicate-tasting mix of veal and pork cold cut.

HEAD CHEESE—a mix of the head meat of calf, pig, or sheep, seasoned and set in gelatin.

LACHSSCHINKEN—dry-cured, boneless, and very lean pork loin.

NUREMBERG SAUSAGES—long, thin, herb-seasoned sausages.

PLOCKWURST—brown, shiny-skinned beef and pork sausage.

SCHINKENWURST—hearty-textured sausage made of beef and pork.

ZUNGENWURST—blood sausages containing chunks of diced pork and tongue; for serious sausage lovers.

Ein Souper heut uns winkt,

A supper beckons us,

Wie noch gar keins dagewesen;

The best ever,

Delikat, auserlesen

The choicest delicacies

Immer hier man speist und trinkt.

Are always eaten and drunk here.

DIE FLEDERMAUS

BACK ROW, LEFT TO RIGHT: **Landjaeger, onions, bratwurst, Herb and Garlic Mustard, Horseradish Honey Mustard.** FRONT ROW, LEFT TO RIGHT: **Wuerzburger, lachsschinken, Cranberry Mustard, krakauer, blutwurst**

CHARCUTERIE PLATTER WITH THREE HOMEMADE MUSTARDS
Serves 8 to 10

The three easy-to-make mustards—forceful horseradish-honey, flavorful herb-garlic, and spicy-sweet cranberry—are perfect with these onion sausages. Just whirl a few ingredients together in a food processor and you have your own delicious homemade mustards in minutes. They last for weeks and taste even better with age. You'll never buy ready-made mustard again.

- ½ pound smoked bacon, diced
- 3 pounds assorted uncooked German sausages such as bratwurst
- 3 large red onions, thinly sliced
- 1 teaspoon caraway seeds
- 4 juniper berries, lightly crushed
- 1 bay leaf
- ½ teaspoon freshly milled black pepper
- ½ cup beer
- 1 to 2 pounds assorted precooked sausages such as knackwurst
- 1 to 2 pounds assorted German cold cuts such as lachsschinken
- Assorted hearty grain and black breads

In a large heavy-bottomed pot, sauté the bacon over medium-high heat until the fat is rendered. Add the uncooked sausages and brown on all sides. Remove the sausages, place on a plate, and cover to keep warm.

Add the onions, caraway seeds, juniper berries, bay leaf, and pepper and sauté until the onions are golden, about 5 minutes. Stir in the beer and return the sausages to the pot. Cover and simmer on low for 20 minutes, or until the sausages are cooked through.

Meanwhile, place the assorted precooked sausages onto a broiler pan and broil for a minute or two per side until warm.

Slice the broiled sausages and arrange them on a large serving platter or cutting board. Slice the onion-cooked sausages and arrange them on the platter topped with the onions. Add the assorted cold cuts and assorted breads to the platter. Serve with homemade mustards.

HORSERADISH HONEY MUSTARD
Makes about ½ cup

- 2 tablespoons prepared horseradish
- 1 tablespoon mustard powder
- 2 tablespoons honey
- ½ teaspoon salt
- ¼ cup extra-virgin olive oil

Combine the horseradish, mustard powder, honey, and salt in a small food processor and puree until well combined. Slowly pulse in the oil until creamy and well incorporated.

Serve in a small decorative bowl.

> *"We must seize our chance and honestly seek to cultivate the age's new forms, and he will be its master who writes in neither an Italian nor a French—nor even in a German—style."*
>
> **RICHARD WAGNER,**
> *German Opera (1834)*

HERB AND GARLIC MUSTARD
Makes about 1 cup

- 2 tablespoons yellow mustard seeds
- 2 tablespoons brown mustard seeds
- 2 tablespoons minced fresh parsley, or 1 teaspoon dried
- 2 tablespoons minced fresh thyme, or 1 teaspoon dried
- 2 tablespoons minced fresh marjoram, or 1 teaspoon dried
- ¼ cup extra-virgin olive oil
- 3 tablespoons red wine vinegar
- 2 to 3 cloves garlic, minced
- 1 teaspoon salt
- 1 teaspoon sugar
- ½ teaspoon freshly milled black pepper

Combine the yellow and brown mustard seeds in a clean coffee grinder and process until finely ground.

Transfer the ground seeds to a small food processor and add the remaining ingredients. Pulse until well combined. The mustard will be thick, so you may need to scrape the sides and pulse again to incorporate all the ingredients.

Serve in a small decorative bowl.

CRANBERRY MUSTARD
Makes about ½ cup

- 3 tablespoons dried cranberries or cherries
- 3 tablespoons pear or raspberry vinegar
- ¼ cup extra-virgin olive oil
- 2 tablespoons brown or yellow mustard seeds
- 1 tablespoon mustard powder
- Salt and freshly milled black pepper

Puree the cranberries and vinegar in a small food processor until the cranberries are finely minced. Add the oil, mustard seeds, and mustard powder and puree until well combined. Season to taste with salt and pepper.

Serve in a small decorative bowl.

OPERA NOTE

Richard Wagner's works *Die Meistersinger von Nürnberg, Tristan und Isolde, Siegfried, Götterdämmerung, Das Rheingold,* and *Parsifal* enjoyed their American premieres at the Metropolitan Opera House.

Wagner's disciple Anton Seidl conducted each of these premieres and brought together the four separate operas of the Ring cycle for their first production in the United States, in 1889, at the Met. Such triumphs were a natural result of Seidl's musical immersion. During his time in Germany, he lived the music so thoroughly that he sometimes corrected errors in the scores before Wagner did. Such devotion left Wagner smitten: "What would I do without my Seidl?" But before one accuses the German giant of excessive sentimentality, they should be let in on the joke: *Seidel* means "beer mug" in German.

MUSTARD HOLDERS

Mustard holders are wonderful collectibles. The oldest mustard pots are rare and date to the fourteenth century, but the average collector can readily find reasonably priced eighteenth- and nineteenth-century containers made in porcelain, pottery, silver, gold, wood, or even glass. Mustard was so popular that in the nineteenth century, a special cruet came about. This combination salt and pepper shaker holder also had small mustard bowls, often covered with hinged lids notched to accommodate the mustard spoon.

If you collect, this German charcuterie platter would be an ideal time to display your mustard pots on the buffet table.

First Course

Napkins have a fascinating history. While it is true that an ancient Roman host would provide basins of water and large towel-like cloths for guests to wash and dry their hands between courses, the real history of the napkin starts in the early Middle Ages.

At first, dirty hands were wiped on the lower edges of the tablecloth, which was provided exactly for that purpose. Starting in the thirteenth century, special wiping cloths were hung on the walls behind the banqueting table. It's from there that the custom of individual napkins took hold in the late Middle Ages. In the 1700s cleverly folding napkins into shapes like fans or swans became popular. Those napkins were larger than the ones we use today. Even as recently as the mid-1800s, they were thirty inches square. By the 1920s, three napkin sizes were popular: small for breakfast or tea, medium-sized for lunch, and large for dinner.

Looking through etiquette books or at still-life paintings of the sixteenth and seventeenth centuries, we see that white damask cloth was dominant. Brightly colored tablecloths and napkins did not become popular until the 1800s. In those days, napkins and tablecloths had to match.

Fortunately, today color is in and matching is out. Just as we don't match our shoes to handbags anymore, neither do we match napkins and tablecloths. Anything goes—theatrical velvets, tapestries, and even Chinese rugs all make acceptable and dramatic table coverings.

Ich lade gern mir Gäste ein,

One lives quite well at my house,

Man lebt bei mir recht fein,

I like to invite guests,

Man unterhält sich, wie man mag

One enjoys oneself, as he likes

Oft bis zum hellen Tag!

Often until the light of day!

DIE FLEDERMAUS

GERMAN SOUR CHERRY SOUP
Serves 4

Wagner often said, "I write with an exclamation point!" Well, this is soup with an exclamation point! Burgundy-colored, tart-sweet, and wine-kissed, it's like romance in a bowl.

Savory fruit soups like this elegant starter are popular throughout northern Europe. I've tried dozens of variations, and this is far and away the best.

- 1 cup best-quality vegetable or chicken stock
- 3 cups pitted sour cherries, fresh, jarred, or frozen
- 1³/4 cups red wine
- One 2-inch stick of cinnamon
- 2 egg yolks, beaten
- Salt and freshly milled black pepper
- 1 cup crème fraîche or sour cream, for serving
- Zest of 1 lemon, for serving
- Freshly grated nutmeg, for serving

Kiri Te Kanawa in *Die Fledermaus*

In a medium saucepan over high heat, bring the stock to a boil. Reduce the heat to medium and add the cherries, 1½ cups of the wine, and the cinnamon stick. Simmer for about 12 minutes, until the cherries are soft. Remove the cinnamon. Allow to cool slightly.

Puree the soup in a blender until very smooth. Return it to the saucepan and whisk in the egg yolks. Simmer on low, whisking occasionally, for about 5 minutes, until the yolks are cooked and the soup is warm. Do not allow the soup to boil, as that would curdle the yolks.

Remove the pan from the heat. Season to taste with salt and pepper and stir in the remaining ¼ cup of wine.

Serve warm with a dollop of crème fraîche, a sprinkle of zest, and a generous topping of freshly grated nutmeg. (Note: Don't even think of using ground nutmeg. If you don't have whole nutmeg, don't use anything.)

OPERA NOTE

Die Fledermaus contains several charming drinking and eating scenes. Act I starts with a cozy supper where Alfred sings to his lover, Rosalinde, encouraging her to forget their disloyalty to her husband: *"Trinke, Liebchen, trinke schnell"*—"Drink, darling, drink quickly." Act II focuses on a party at Prince Orlofsky's palace, where the guests sing of the splendor of the prince's offerings and dub him "Champagne the First."

Second Course

IN RICHARD STRAUSS'S *DIE FRAU OHNE SCHATTEN*, the nurse amazes the dyer's wife by clapping her hands to send fish flying through the air into a blazing skillet. While this dish won't make itself quite so magically as the nurse's, it is a foolproof method that always results in a tender and moist trout.

TROUT WITH ROASTED MEYER LEMONS
Serves 4

As an accompaniment serve slow-roasted lemons, which can be eaten whole, skin and all. Meyer lemons, smaller and sweeter than regular lemons, are ideal in this recipe and are available in the States from November through May. Regular lemons are fine too.

This dish goes well with boiled red potatoes or wedges of black bread.

- 4 Meyer or regular lemons
- 4 tablespoons sugar
- 3 tablespoons unsalted butter
- 1 onion, thinly sliced
- 1 carrot, grated
- 1/2 cup minced fresh dill, plus fronds for garnish
- 2 tablespoons white wine vinegar
- Salt and freshly milled black pepper
- 4 trout, cleaned and boned
- 1/2 cup all-purpose flour
- 3 tablespoons olive oil
- 1 cup white wine
- 4 bay leaves
- Freshly squeezed juice and zest of 2 lemons

Preheat the oven to 250°F.

Place each lemon on its own large square of aluminum foil and sprinkle it with 1 tablespoon sugar. Tightly wrap each lemon in the foil and place it onto a baking sheet. Bake for about 1 hour, until the lemons are very tender. Leave them to cool in their foil on the baking sheet as they will release juices during the process.

In a large sauté pan over medium heat, melt the butter and cook the onion until golden. Stir in the carrot, dill, and vinegar. Season to taste with salt and pepper. Reserve.

Liberally season the trout inside and out with salt and pepper. Place 1/4 of the onion mixture inside each trout and close with two wooden toothpicks. Dredge the trout in the flour.

Heat the oil in the same large sauté pan over medium-high heat. Add the trout, and cook for 2 minutes per side.

Pour 1/2 cup of the wine into the pan, add the bay leaves, and cook for 2 minutes, or until the wine evaporates. Carefully turn the trout once more, pour the remaining 1/2 cup of wine, the lemon juice, and the zest on top of the trout, and cook for about 1 minute.

Place the trout on a serving platter. Garnish with dill fronds and the baked lemons. Pour the juices released by the lemons over the fish.

Fischlein fünf aus Fischers Zuber,

Fishes five from the fisher's pail

Wandert ins öl!

Into the oil!

Und, Pfanne, empfang sie!

Frying pan, receive them!

Feuer, rühr dich!

Fire, blaze up!

DIE FRAU OHNE SCHATTEN

Die Majestät wird anerkannt,

His majesty is acknowledged,

Anerkannt rings im Land;

Acknowledged throughout the land;

Jubelnd wird Champagner

He is jubilantly crowned

Der Erste sie genannt!

Champagne the First!

Es lebe Champagner der Erste!

Long live Champagne the First!

DIE FLEDERMAUS

Tatiana Troyanos in *Die Fledermaus*

WHITE ASPARAGUS WITH STRAWBERRY CHAMPAGNE VINAIGRETTE
Serves 6

Strawberries and champagne—a classic combination—create an elegant vinaigrette that would have starred at Prince Orlofsky's table. The strawberries are pureed in a blender with the other dressing ingredients, which turns the vinaigrette a lovely color, especially when topped with pink peppercorns. The dressing is particularly striking against the stark white asparagus but is gorgeous on any salad.

- **1 bunch white asparagus, ends trimmed**
- **Salt**
- **6 medium-sized strawberries, chopped**
- **3 tablespoons champagne vinegar**
- **¾ cup grape seed or olive oil**
- **1 teaspoon whole pink peppercorns, plus more for garnish**
- **¼ cup champagne**

Blanch the asparagus in a skillet in a small amount of salted water. Drain and reserve.

In a small food processor, puree the strawberries and vinegar until smooth. Slowly pulse in the oil and peppercorns until very creamy, then sir in the champagne. Season to taste with salt.

Arrange the asparagus on a serving platter. Place the vinaigrette in a decorative dipping bowl or drizzle it over the asparagus. Garnish with a few peppercorns.

Main Course

PERHAPS YOU WANT TO TEST OUT A RECIPE but you're not sure how it will turn out or if anyone will like it. What do you do? My suggestion is to serve it in appetizer-sized portions.

Instead of serving a new dish as a main course, I cut the recipe in half and serve it as one of the starters. If it's a flop, the damage is minimal—there's still the main course to come. You'll be surprised how much fun you and your guests can have. People enjoy participating as test subjects!

So don't be afraid to try new things; just do it in small doses. The following recipe for venison stew is a perfect candidate for the appetizer strategy. The sauce is so thick that it sticks to the succulent chunks of venison speared onto sturdy toothpicks.

HERE'S ANOTHER WAY TO EXPERIMENT WITH NEW DISHES

Serve two different versions of the same recipe to different sides of the table. The guests can taste one another's food and give opinions. My friends all say they appreciate becoming part of the process. Try it!

Testing new dishes with guests also has a psychological benefit. A lot of hosts become nervous with company coming. This may be one reason that Thanksgiving and other holiday dinners can be stressful. By announcing in advance that you are experimenting, you immediately lower the stakes, making it clear that you're not perfect and that you want input. This can be very liberating and preempts criticism. (It works particularly well with judgmental people—in-laws, for example!) I'm a psychologist by training. Interestingly, since becoming a professional cookbook author and food writer, I've found that I use more psychology than ever.

OPERA NOTE

Richard Wagner's legacy includes not only great operas, but theater design as well.

In the Bayreuth Festspielhaus, which he built, Wagner removed box seats so everyone had an unobstructed view of the stage. To further focus the audience's attention, he recessed the orchestra into the "pit" we know today.

Finally, Wagner was the first ever to darken the house lights. We take a darkened theater so much for granted nowadays, but before Wagner's 1876 innovation, theater interiors were brightly lit so that patrons could see each other and read librettos.

DER FREISCHÜTZ VENISON STEW WITH TWO WINES
Serves 8

When dried plums are slow-cooked, they dissolve, creating a gorgeous purple-ebony sauce that is delicately sweet with a complex flavor. Venison cooked in this sauce leaves no trace of gaminess. I promise.

The secret to the dish is the two wines. The meat is marinated in Riesling, which connoisseurs consider one of the world's best wines. Its spicy, fruity flavor marinates the meat to mellow perfection. Red wine is then added in the cooking to develop an exquisitely rich sauce.

- 2 cups Riesling wine
- 2 large Vidalia onions, thinly sliced
- 3 large sprigs fresh rosemary
- 2 tablespoons fresh minced ginger
- 1 tablespoon whole black peppercorns
- 1 tablespoon juniper berries, lightly crushed
- 1 tablespoon whole allspice
- 1 teaspoon whole cloves
- One 2-inch stick of cinnamon
- 3 bay leaves
- 5 blades of mace
- 3 pounds venison shoulder, cut into 1½-inch cubes
- Salt and freshly milled black pepper
- ¾ pound smoked bacon, diced
- 1 cup red wine
- 4 cloves garlic, minced
- 2 cups diced dried plums or prunes
- One 8-ounce jar ready-roasted chestnuts
- ¼ cup finely minced fresh parsley, for serving

Bring the Riesling to a low boil over medium heat in a medium saucepan. Add 1 of the onions, the rosemary, ginger, peppercorns, juniper berries, allspice, cloves, cinnamon, bay leaves, and mace and simmer for 15 minutes.

Cool to room temperature, then combine this marinade with the venison in a bowl. Cover with plastic wrap and refrigerate overnight.

Remove the venison from the marinade. Strain the marinade, discarding the solids but reserving the liquid.

Season the venison with salt and pepper to taste.

In a large, heavy-bottomed stockpot over medium heat, sauté the bacon for about 3 minutes until the fat is rendered. Add the venison and the remaining onion and sauté for about 5 minutes. Add the reserved marinade liquid, red wine, garlic, dried plums, and chestnuts.

Cover and reduce the heat to low. Simmer for 1½ hours, until the meat is very tender. Season to taste with salt and pepper. Serve hot, topped with parsley.

Pilar Lorengar and Sándor Kónya in *Der Freischütz*

SPAETZLE WITH SPINACH NUTMEG BUTTER
Serves 4 to 6

Flavored butter is easy and fun to make. Here, creamy sweet butter is accented with savory shallots, spinach, and gloriously fragrant nutmeg. The seasonings blend to create gorgeous green-flecked rounds. It's not only delectable but also beautiful; try it with rice or egg noodles, as well as spaetzle.

Spaetzle, meaning "little sparrow" in German, is one of that country's traditional side dishes.

- **2 tablespoons olive oil**
- **1 shallot, minced**
- **2 cups fresh spinach**
- **½ cup (1 stick) unsalted butter, softened**
- **1 teaspoon freshly grated nutmeg, plus more as garnish**
- **Salt and freshly milled black pepper**
- **1 pound dry prepared spaetzle**
- **½ cup freshly grated Parmesan cheese**

In a small sauté pan over medium heat, heat the oil and cook the shallot until soft, about 2 minutes. Add the spinach, cover, and cook for a minute or two until wilted. Allow to cool. Puree in a small food processor.

In a bowl, combine the spinach puree with the butter and nutmeg until smooth. Season to taste with salt and pepper.

Place the butter mixture on an 18-inch-long section of plastic wrap and form it into a 6-inch log. Wrap the plastic around the butter and twist the ends closed. Press to form an even log shape. Refrigerate for about 3 hours, or until firm.

Meanwhile, cook the spaetzle according to package directions. Drain and toss with the cheese. Top each portion with several slices of the butter and a sprinkle of nutmeg.

OPERA NOTE

The prologue of *Ariadne auf Naxos*, set in the home of the wealthiest man in Vienna, revolves around planning the entertainments for that evening's banquet—a very realistic flurry of last-minute details every modern-day host can relate to.

> *"Achievements, seldom credited to their source, are the result of unspeakable drudgery and worries."*
>
> **RICHARD WAGNER**

Von Freias Frucht

Of Freia's fruit

Genosset ihr heute noch nicht:

You've not yet eaten today.

Die goldnen Äpfel

The golden apples

In ihrem Garten,

That grow in her garden,

Sie machten euch tüchtig und jung,

They kept you so vigorous and young,

Aßt ihr sie jeden Tag.

Eating them every day.

DAS RHEINGOLD

FREIA'S GOLDEN APPLES WITH KALE
Serves 4 to 6

Bright purple-green kale substitutes for its country cousin, cabbage, to make an elegant version of the traditional sweet-and-sour German cabbage side dish.

The apples and honey add wonderful sweetness, while vinegar and caraway provide just the right hint of tartness.

1 large red onion, thinly sliced

1 tablespoon olive oil

2 tablespoons unsalted butter

2 Golden Delicious apples, cored and sliced

2 to 3 tablespoons pear or raspberry vinegar

2 tablespoons honey

1 teaspoon caraway seeds

1 bunch purple kale, chopped

Salt and freshly milled black pepper

In a large skillet over medium heat, sauté the onion in the oil and butter until golden, about 5 minutes. Add the apples, vinegar, honey, and caraway seeds and sauté 2 to 3 minutes, until the apples are tender.

Add the kale, cover, and sauté until the kale is tender, about 3 minutes. Season to taste with salt and pepper, and serve.

OPERA NOTE

The Metropolitan Opera House's early years so focused on German works that even many Italian operas were performed in German. Wagner was by far the favorite, with ten of his operas staged in the 1889–1890 season alone.

Dessert

DRIED ORANGE PEEL, FEATURED IN ISOLDE'S MARZIPAN KISSES, can be found in the spice rack of most supermarkets. It's great in all sorts of cookies and cakes, and especially in chocolate recipes. It can be added to the batter and sprinkled on top of sweets. A teaspoonful in vinaigrettes, soups, or stews adds a lovely citrus tang.

FLOURLESS APRICOT POPPY SEED CAKE
Serves 10 to 12

This lighter-than-air, poppy seed–studded cake, with a hint of citrus and tang of apricots, is a scrumptious update of the traditional German poppy seed treat, *Mohnkuchen*.

1 cup blanched almonds

1/2 cup (1 stick) unsalted butter, plus additional for the pan

1/2 cup plus 2 tablespoons sugar

Zest of 1/2 orange

6 large eggs, separated

1 1/4 cups ground poppy seeds

1 cup minced dried apricots

2 tablespoons finely minced best-quality candied orange peel

2 tablespoons Cointreau or rum

1 teaspoon vanilla extract

Pinch of salt

Confectioners' sugar

Generously butter an 8- or 9-inch springform baking pan and set aside. Preheat the oven to 400°F.

Put the almonds into a small food processor and grind until very fine. Reserve.

In a bowl using an electric mixer, beat the butter, sugar, and zest until creamy. Add the egg yolks, one at a time, blending until well incorporated. Blend in the poppy seeds, ground almonds, apricots, candied orange peel, Cointreau, and vanilla until well combined.

In another bowl using an electric mixer beat the egg whites with the salt until stiff peaks form. Mix a heaping tablespoon of the egg whites into the poppy seed mixture to lighten it and then stir in the remaining whites until just incorporated. Do not overstir.

Pour the batter into the prepared pan and put it into the oven. Immediately reduce the heat to 300°F and bake for 30 to 35 minutes until set.

Serve warm or at room temperature topped with confectioners' sugar.

"Music is a higher revelation than all wisdom and philosophy, it is the wine of a new procreation, and I am Bacchus who presses out this glorious wine for men and makes them drunk with the spirit."

LUDWIG VAN BEETHOVEN

ISOLDE'S MARZIPAN KISSES
Makes about 21 kisses

Marzipan is a German favorite, and you'll just adore what they have done with it here. Ready-made almond paste is flavored with a hint of fragrant rose water and then molded to form tiny balls studded with almond slices. When you press on the almonds, the balls squish in to form tiny kiss-shaped drops, which bake up golden brown. A sprinkle of dried orange peel adds just a hint of tartness, which perfectly balances the sweetness of marzipan.

Not only do these kisses make a wonderful after-dinner sweet, but they stay fresh-tasting for a month, making them a great homemade gift. Pack them in decorative boxes for a present that's like a kiss on the cheek.

Almond paste is sold in most supermarkets in jars or foil-wrapped logs. Be sure to check the expiration date and select fresh almond paste. It should be soft and malleable, with a texture like Play-Doh.

- 7 ounces almond paste
- 2 tablespoons rose water or rose syrup, plus more as needed
- Confectioners' or superfine sugar, if needed
- 1 egg, beaten
- Almond slices
- Dried orange peel

Crumble the almond paste into a small shallow bowl and sprinkle with the rose water. Using your hands, knead the mixture until smooth and silky. Add more rose water, if the dough isn't moist enough.

Taste a pinch of the dough and add sugar, if you like. Some almond pastes are already sweetened, so it may not need sugar.

Take teaspoon-sized sections of the dough and roll each in your hands to form a small ball. Press the balls on a parchment- or silpat-lined cookie sheet so they are flattened on the bottom.

Using a pastry brush, generously coat the balls with egg. A generous coating of egg is the key to achieving a nice golden-brown color.

Firmly press 3 almond slices into each ball, evenly spacing them around the ball. This three-sided pressing will cause the ball to form into a "kiss" droplike shape.

Again using a pastry brush, generously coat the almond surfaces and the rest of the kiss with the beaten egg. Top with a sprinkle of dried orange peel. Allow the kisses to dry uncovered overnight or for at least 6 hours. (If you don't have time to wait for the kisses to dry, you can bake them immediately. The results will be chewier and less cookie-like but still outstanding.)

Bake the kisses in a preheated 300°F oven for about 20 minutes, until golden. Allow to cool completely before removing them from the cookie sheet.

Birgit Nilsson and Mignon Dunn in *Tristan und Isolde*

Chapter Five

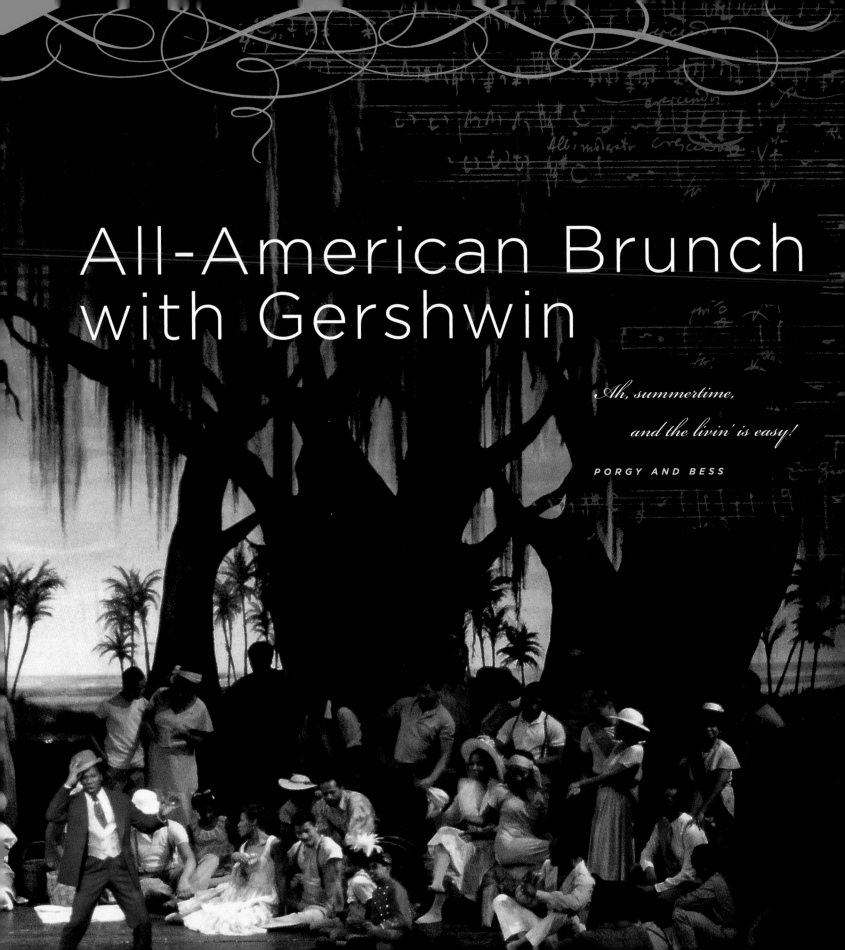

All-American Brunch with Gershwin

Ah, summertime,
and the livin' is easy!
PORGY AND BESS

This chapter celebrates the American composer George Gershwin with a meal featuring some of our nation's finest artisanal products—handmade cheeses, heirloom tomatoes, maple syrup, crisp fall apples, and country ham. ⤜∽

The brunch menu is inspired by George Gershwin's opera, *Porgy and Bess*. Start with the creamy Southern favorite, Charleston Peanut Soup, accompanied by a refreshing Sparkling Apple Harvest Cocktail made with sparkling wine, apple cider, and a hint of orange liqueur. Follow with a Country Ham Breakfast Casserole with Crispy Chive Onion Rings, assembled the night before so you can relax over the Sunday paper while it bakes. This goes great alongside Melt-in-Your-Mouth Maple Buttermilk Biscuits, a fragrant, maple-sweet treat.

Menu

COCKTAILS

Sparkling Apple Harvest Cocktail

Heirloom Tomato Cocktail

STARTERS

Charleston Peanut Soup

American Artisanal Cheeses with
Mint Julep Jam and Bloody Mary Marmalade

BRUNCH

Melt-in-Your-Mouth Maple Buttermilk Biscuits

Apple and Butternut Squash "Hash" with
Southern Comfort

Country Ham Breakfast Casserole with
Crispy Chive Onion Rings

Porgy's Peach Ice Cream

PREVIOUS PAGES: *Porgy and Bess*

Cocktails

Apples are lovely—bright yellow Honey Golds, green Granny Smiths, ruby Red Delicious, multitone Pink Lady apples, all echoing the brilliant colors of fall. Fill glass bowls or vases with an apple assortment to elegantly decorate a room.

Continue the apple theme with whimsical Lady apple name cards. Write the guest's name on a piece of paper, such as sticky address labels artistically printed, and then attach them to a toothpick. Insert the toothpick into the center of the Lady apple and you have an edible place card holder!

SPARKLING APPLE HARVEST COCKTAIL
Serves 1

There are many fine American sparkling whites that substitute perfectly well for French Champagne. Examples are Iron Horse Sonoma Blanc de Blancs and Mumm Cuvée M. This mixture of American sparkling wine, apple cider, and a splash of orange liqueur will wake you up in style.

    ½ ounce fresh apple cider
    Splash of orange liqueur such as Cointreau
    American sparkling white wine
    Apple slice or candied orange peel section,
        for garnish

Pour the apple cider and orange liqueur into a fluted champagne glass and top with wine. Serve with an apple slice or slice of candied orange peel.

HEIRLOOM TOMATO COCKTAIL
Serves 1

Once you try heirloom tomato juice in your Bloody Mary, you'll never be satisfied with anything less.

    ¾ cup diced heirloom tomatoes
    1 ounce vodka
    ¼ teaspoon Worcestershire sauce
    ½ teaspoon fresh minced dill
    Dash of Tabasco
    Freshly squeezed juice of ¼ lemon
    Salt and freshly milled black pepper
    1 celery stalk, for garnish
    1 carrot stick, for garnish

In a blender, mix the tomatoes, vodka, Worcestershire, dill, Tabasco, lemon juice, and salt and pepper to taste until smooth. Pour over ice into an old-fashioned or short glass. Garnish with the celery and carrot.

APPLE TASTING

Winesap apples get their name because they have the lovely aroma of fine red wine. Approach tasting an apple as you would a glass of fine wine.

Take a moment to notice the apple's unique color and fragrance. Chew the first bite v-e-r-y slowly. Notice the texture and nuances of taste. For instance, some apples have hints of other fruit flavors, like grapes or raspberries. After the first bite, notice the apple's aromas, which can include flower scents like violets or roses.

Starters

SHOW OFF YOUR AMERICANA COLLECTIBLES at a brunch celebrating America's composers. Substitute a quilt for your usual tablecloth, bring out your Depression glass and Fiestaware, and decorate the tabletop with other favorite pieces of Americana. Whimsical salt- and pepper shakers from the '40s, charming napkin rings from the turn of the century, and vintage Pez dispensers all make lovely centerpiece arrangements and are great conversation starters.

OPERA NOTE

DuBose Heyward, author of the novel *Porgy* and Gershwin's collaborator on the opera, lived across the street from Cabbage Row in Charleston, South Carolina, which became Catfish Row in the novel, play, and opera. The real-life setting got its name because shopkeepers and tenants peddled vegetables from their stands and windowsills.

The folks living in Gershwin's Catfish Row speak Gullah, a rapid-fire rhythmic dialect common in many parts of the South, especially in South Carolina. Part Elizabethan English and part African, Gullah has given us such words as *gumbo* and also *goober*, for peanuts.

CHARLESTON PEANUT SOUP
Serves 8

A spoonful of Southern hospitality, creamy yet surprisingly light, this soup bursts with flavor. You'll love the combination of sweet potatoes, peanuts, spicy cayenne, tangy lime, and fragrant cilantro.

2 tablespoons peanut or vegetable oil

1 large onion, chopped

1 large sweet potato, peeled and cubed

1 cup unsalted peanuts, plus more, chopped, for garnish

¼ cup creamy peanut butter

5 cups best-quality chicken or vegetable stock

Freshly squeezed juice and grated zest of 1 lime

Salt and freshly milled black pepper

Cayenne

Chopped cilantro, for garnish

Heat the oil in a large, heavy-bottomed saucepan over medium heat, and sauté the onion for 10 minutes, until golden. Stir in the sweet potato, peanuts, peanut butter, and stock and bring to a boil. Cover, reduce the heat to low, and cook until the potatoes are very soft, about 30 minutes.

Allow to cool slightly and, working in small batches, puree the soup in a blender. Transfer it back to the saucepan and stir in the lime juice and salt, pepper, and cayenne to taste.

To serve, ladle the soup into bowls and garnish with the lime zest, cilantro, and chopped peanuts.

AMERICAN ARTISANAL CHEESES WITH MINT JULEP JAM AND BLOODY MARY MARMALADE
Serves 6 to 8

Wildly flavorful, these easy-to-make whimsical jams elevate a cheese platter to new heights. The Mint Julep Jam pairs wonderfully with sharp cheese to mellow it, while adding a nice bourbon kick. Spicy Bloody Mary Marmalade is great with mild or creamy cheeses for a pleasing level of flavor contrasts.

Try an assortment of American artisanal cheeses like Berkshire Blue cheese, Cowgirl Creamery's triple-cream Mt. Tam, Vermont Shepherd, or dry Monterey Jack from the Vella Cheese Company.

A simple rule of thumb is to serve at least three cheeses and plan on two ounces each per guest.

- ¼ cup bourbon
- ½ cup sugar
- Freshly squeezed juice of 2 lemons
- 1 cup fresh mint leaves
- ¼ cup vodka
- 1 cup diced heirloom or vine-ripened tomatoes
- ½ teaspoon Worcestershire sauce
- Dash of Tabasco
- Salt and freshly milled black pepper
- 1 pound assorted cheeses

For the jam, in a medium saucepan, heat the bourbon, sugar, and half of the lemon juice over a low flame until thickened, about 3 minutes. Allow to cool. Puree with the mint in a food processor or blender until well combined. Reserve in a small serving bowl.

For the marmalade, in a medium saucepan over medium heat, simmer the vodka, tomatoes, Worcestershire, Tabasco, and remaining lemon juice for about 10 minutes until thickened. Season to taste with salt and pepper. Reserve in a small serving bowl.

Arrange the cheeses on a serving platter along with the Mint Julep Jam and Bloody Mary Marmalade.

Mervin Wallace and Priscilla Baskerville in *Porgy and Bess*

"A great American opera should be in the repertory of the great American opera house."

JAMES LEVINE,
on *Porgy and Bess*

Brunch

MELT-IN-YOUR-MOUTH MAPLE BUTTERMILK BISCUITS
Serves 6

The tantalizing aroma of these biscuits fills your kitchen with the feeling of South Carolina sunshine. If you're trying to sell your home, bake these just before prospective buyers visit. Sold!

- 2 cups all-purpose flour
- 2 tablespoons maple sugar
- 1 teaspoon baking powder
- 1 teaspoon salt
- 1/2 teaspoon baking soda
- 6 tablespoons cold unsalted butter, cut into small pieces
- 3/4 cup buttermilk

Preheat the oven to 400°F. Line a baking sheet with parchment paper and set aside.

In a large bowl, stir together the flour, maple sugar, baking powder, salt, and baking soda until well combined. Work in the butter with a fork and then add the buttermilk. Stir just until the dough comes together.

Pat the dough out into a 6-inch circle and cut it into 6 pie-shaped wedges. Transfer them to the baking sheet and bake for about 12 minutes, or until golden.

Serve warm.

APPLE AND BUTTERNUT SQUASH "HASH" WITH SOUTHERN COMFORT
Serves 6

Toasted sesame oil gives the butternut squash a lovely golden color and rich nutty flavor. The splash of Southern Comfort, which is a mix of bourbon and peaches, and the tangy cranberries make this dish sublime. If you have any left over, which is unlikely, use it as a spread on turkey or chicken sandwiches.

- 1/2 cup dried cranberries
- 1/2 cup Southern Comfort bourbon
- 1 butternut squash, peeled, seeded, and diced
- 3 tablespoons toasted sesame oil
- 1/4 cup best-quality chicken stock
- 1 Granny Smith apple, diced
- 5 or 6 sprigs fresh thyme
- Salt and freshly milled black pepper

In a small bowl, soak the cranberries in the bourbon for at least 30 minutes or up to 24 hours.

In a large skillet over high heat, sauté the squash in the oil until golden, about 6 minutes. Lower the heat to medium, add the bourbon cranberries, and cook, stirring, until the bourbon is absorbed. Add the stock, apple, and thyme, cover, and simmer for about 6 minutes until the squash is tender. Season to taste with salt and pepper.

COUNTRY HAM BREAKFAST CASSEROLE WITH CRISPY CHIVE ONION RINGS
Serves 8

Assemble the ingredients for this casserole the night before. In the morning, just pop it into the oven and enjoy absolute perfection. The ham and gooey cheese gets just the right crunch from the chive-accented crispy onion rings. An absolutely magical way to use leftover bread.

10 eggs

1½ cups half-and-half

Salt and freshly milled black pepper

Unsalted butter, for the pan

1 large loaf crusty bread or mix of breads, cut into 1-inch slices

2 pounds cooked country ham, coarsely chopped

1 large red onion, minced

1 pound Cheddar cheese, grated

¼ cup honey

1 large white onion, sliced into thin rounds

½ cup heavy cream

1 cup all-purpose flour

2 tablespoons finely minced fresh chives

Peanut or vegetable oil, for frying

In a medium bowl, whisk the eggs with the half-and-half and salt and pepper to taste. Reserve.

Butter a 9-by-13-inch baking pan. Line the pan with one layer of bread and top with the ham, red onion, three quarters of the cheese and the honey. Pour on half the egg mixture. Top with a final layer of bread and the rest of the egg mixture. Cover and refrigerate overnight.

Preheat the oven to 350°F. Cook, covered, for about 30 minutes, or until the egg mixture is set.

Meanwhile, prepare the crispy chive onion rings. In a large bowl toss the onion rings with the cream until well coated. In another bowl, whisk together the flour, chives, and salt and pepper to taste.

Heat 1 inch of oil in a large frying pan over medium-high heat. Working in small batches, remove the onion rings from the cream, dredge in the flour mixture, and fry, until golden, about 2 minutes per side. Transfer the onion rings to a paper-towel-lined plate to drain excess oil. Add more oil, as needed, to finish cooking all the onion rings.

Raise the heat to broil. Remove the cover, sprinkle with the remaining cheese, and broil until the cheese is golden, about 1 minute. Serve the breakfast casserole topped with the onion rings.

PORGY'S PEACH ICE CREAM
Serves 6, makes about 1 quart

This quick-to-prepare classic Southern treat can be made without an ice cream machine.

$\frac{1}{2}$ **cup sugar**

2 cups sliced fresh peaches, about 1 pound

2 teaspoons freshly squeezed lemon juice

1 cup heavy cream

In a large bowl, sprinkle the sugar over the peaches. Stir gently and set aside for 30 minutes.

In a blender or food processor, puree the sugared peaches until very smooth. Blend in the lemon juice and cream until well combined.

Pour into a freezerproof container, cover, and freeze for about 2 hours until almost frozen. Put the mixture back into the food processor or blender and puree again. Return it to the freezerproof container, cover, and freeze until hardened.

OPERA NOTE

The Metropolitan Opera House has presented the world premieres of many operas by American composers. While John Corigliano's *The Ghosts of Versailles* (1991) has a particularly French theme, Philip Glass's *The Voyage* (1992), commemorating the five-hundredth anniversary of Columbus's journey, and John Harbison's *The Great Gatsby* (1999) are works in a decidedly American spirit. Tobias Picker's *An American Tragedy*, based on Theodore Dreiser's novel about an American dream gone horribly awry, continued in this vein with its premiere on December 2, 2005.

OPERA NOTE

The first American opera to be performed at the Met was *The Pipe of Desire*, by Frederick Converse, on March 18, 1910. *Mona*, by Horatio Parker, was the first American work commissioned by the Met. It was performed in 1912.

Simon Estes and company in Catfish Row in *Porgy and Bess*

OPERA NOTE

The first woman to conduct at the Met was
Sarah Caldwell in 1976. She had founded
the Opera Company of Boston in 1957 and
headed it until its demise in 1991.

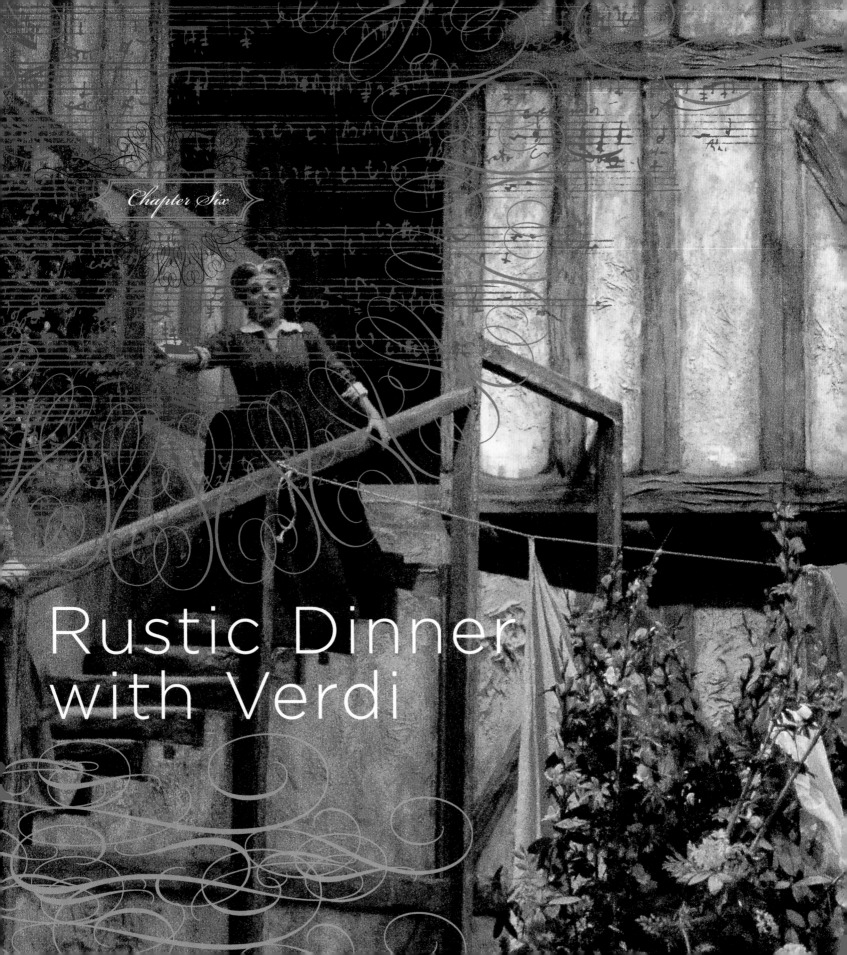

Chapter Six

Rustic Dinner
with Verdi

Tutto nel mondo é burla

All the world's a jest.

L'uom é nato burlone,

Man is born a clown.

La fede in cor gli ciurla,

His faith falters
in his heart;

Gli ciurla la ragione,

His reason wavers
within him.

Tutti gabbati! Irride

We've all been mocked!
Every mortal

L'un l'altro ogni mortal.

Laughs at everyone else!

Ma ride ben chi ride

But he who has
the best laugh

La risata final.

Is he who laughs last.

FALSTAFF

THIS CHAPTER CELEBRATES GIUSEPPE VERDI'S OPERAS with classic foods from the region of his birth, Italy's Po Valley. You'll delight in tasting Falstaff's Fig and Prosciutto Penne, highlighting the most famous ingredients of the area: Parmesan cheese and prosciutto di Parma. Savor Insalata Russa, a dish created by Italians as a tribute to Russian cuisine and a fitting complement to *La Forza del Destino*, Verdi's spirited work commissioned by the Russian court. The main course is osso bucco (here whimsically dubbed Osso *Nabucco*) served with an aromatic Herb Risotto, both specialties of Milan. Dinner concludes with a dessert tribute to *Aida*, a pyramid of honey-coated pastry puffs. *Buon Appetito!*

Menu

PRIMI PIATTI
Minestrone alla Traviata
Falstaff's Fig and Prosciutto Penne
Insalata Russa
Focaccia con Rosmarino

SECONDO PIATTO
Osso Nabucco
Herb Risotto

DOLCI
Citrus Honey Pyramid
Amaretto-Rum Balls

Primi Piatti

FOR A RUSTIC EFFECT, bring the color and beauty of the farmer's market into your home. Decorate with gorgeous vegetables instead of flowers. Arrange stems of Brussels sprouts in ceramic pots. Place assorted gourds in a tall glass vase or glass bowl. Display mixed clusters of green and white asparagus tied with ribbon as a vase-less centerpiece.

MINESTRONE ALLA *TRAVIATA*
Serves 6

This is one of the best soups you'll ever taste.

Fresh tomatoes contribute a big part of the soup's flavor. They are only cooked a short time, so you really savor true tomato taste. It may sound like a lot of fuss to blanch, peel, and seed tomatoes, but it makes a huge difference and it's not so much work. Pop the tomatoes into boiling water and the skins sort of fall off by themselves. Don't obsess like my grandmother, who used an espresso spoon to pick out every last seed! Just halve the tomatoes on a cutting board and watch the seeds ooze out on their own.

I've conducted countless taste tests, comparing all sorts of top-quality canned tomatoes, and they do not approach the flavor of fresh heirloom or vine-ripened tomatoes. Careful! If you're thinking of using ordinary rock-hard supermarket tomatoes, then yes, the best canned will be superior. But you shouldn't use those tomatoes, ever!

The dish is a soup version of pasta puttanesca and would have been a fitting first course at one of Violetta's fine dinner parties.

As it simmers and the aromas fill the kitchen, your doorbell is likely to ring. Your neighbors will pretend to need a cup of sugar, but don't be fooled. They are just hoping for a taste!

3 tablespoons extra-virgin olive oil
1 large red onion, minced
2 anchovy fillets
6 cloves garlic, minced
Red pepper flakes
½ cup white wine
2 cups best-quality vegetable or chicken stock

6 to 7 heirloom tomatoes, about 2 pounds, peeled, seeded, and chopped (or one 14½-ounce can of best-quality diced tomatoes such as Muir Glenn fire-roasted diced tomatoes)
20 pitted oil-cured black olives, coarsely chopped
3 tablespoons capers, drained
Salt and freshly milled black pepper
Chopped fresh parsley, for serving
Grated Romano cheese, for serving

Heat the oil in a medium saucepan over medium-low heat. Add the onion and cook 10 minutes, until soft. Add the anchovy, garlic, and red pepper flakes to taste. Using a fork, mash the anchovy fillets until they dissolve. Add the wine, bring to a boil, and then add the stock and tomatoes and cook until the soup just begins to boil. Remove it from the heat and allow to cool enough to transfer to a food processor.

Puree the tomato soup until smooth. Return it to the saucepan and stir in the olives and capers. Season to taste with salt and pepper.

Reheat the soup on low until warm. Serve topped with parsley and a sprinkle of Romano cheese.

"To write good opera you must have the courage not to write."

GIUSEPPE VERDI

FALSTAFF'S FIG AND PROSCIUTTO PENNE
Serves 6

Figs and prosciutto, a classic Italian combination, make a delicious pasta topping. If I could, I would come to your house and feed you a forkful to convince you to make it. It's really a shame that I'm limited to words on a page, but let me try to describe flavor heaven.

Dried figs simmered with wine and stock take on a delightful, complex flavor with pleasing firmness. The silky-sweet fig sauce is tossed with penne and then accented with luscious prosciutto and crunchy pistachios. Their sweetness is balanced with the piquant bite of pink peppercorn and the salty goodness of Parmesan.

I named this must-try dish for Verdi's *Falstaff* because it is based on the rich fruit sauces popular in the Renaissance and Elizabethan eras. It might have even been on the bill of fare at the Garter's Inn!

    ½ cup (1 stick) unsalted butter

    2 tablespoons extra-virgin olive oil

    6 shallots, sliced

    1 cup white wine

    16 to 18 dried Calimyrna figs, about 12 ounces, thinly
        sliced

    1½ cups best-quality canned chicken stock

    1 pound penne

    ¼ pound prosciutto di Parma, sliced paper thin

    ½ cup shaved Parmesan cheese

    ¼ cup pistachio nuts, coarsely crushed

    1 tablespoon whole pink peppercorns

Heat the butter and oil in a medium sauté pan over medium heat until the butter melts. Sauté the shallots until translucent, about 3 minutes.

Add the wine and figs and simmer until the wine is absorbed and the figs are soft, about 8 minutes. Stir in the stock and simmer, covered, for about 7 minutes.

Remove from heat and let rest, covered, while you prepare the penne according to package directions. Drain and toss with the fig sauce.

Serve the penne topped with the prosciutto, Parmesan, and a sprinkle of pistachio nuts and pink peppercorns.

NOTE: You'll notice that I didn't add the usual tag line, "Season to taste with salt and pepper." That's because the dish gets enough salt from the Parmesan and enough heat from the pink peppercorns.

OPERA NOTE

The corner of Broadway and Seventy-second Street in New York City is named for Giuseppe Verdi. But did you know that there's also an asteroid dedicated to him? Discovered in 1982, it was named 3975 Verdi in the maestro's honor.

Asteroids have been named for other opera composers, including 4132 Bartók, 1815 Beethoven, 2055 Dvořák, 3159 Prokofiev, 4345 Rachmaninoff, 2669 Shostakovich, 4559 Strauss, 4382 Stravinsky, 2266 Tchaikovsky, and 4330 Vivaldi.

INSALATA RUSSA
Serves 8 to 10

While researching this book, I was excited to discover that Russia's Czar Alexander II commissioned Verdi's *La Forza del Destino*. That fact became the perfect excuse to include this Italian-invented but Russian-inspired recipe.

Insalata Russa, despite the name, is a totally Italian creation, very popular in Italy, but virtually unknown in the States or even in Russia! In Italy, especially northern Italy, Insalata Russa is one of those homemade dishes that friends prepare for potluck parties. Almost every Italian I know has his own secret recipe.

The salad is basically a chop-and-mix affair. It's made mainly from classic jarred Italian products like capers, cocktail onions, and *giardiniera*—that zesty mix of vinegar-marinated veggies. The magic is in the combination of textures, colors, and tastes. With each bite you're struck with a burst of flavors—crunchy carrots, tangy olives, spicy vinegary red peppers, sweet peas, and all sorts of other good things, all tossed in a creamy tuna-mayonnaise dressing.

- 5 hard-boiled eggs
- Two 6½-ounce cans best-quality oil-packed tuna, drained and flaked
- 1 cup mayonnaise
- Freshly squeezed juice of 1 large lemon
- One 16-ounce jar *giardiniera* pickled vegetable salad, rinsed, drained, and minced
- 1 cup frozen baby peas, defrosted
- One 3-ounce jar capers, drained, about ½ cup
- One 5-ounce jar cocktail onions, rinsed and drained
- 1 carrot, minced
- 1 stalk celery, minced
- 1 large russet potato, boiled, peeled, and chopped
- 12 Sicilian olives, pitted and chopped
- 3 tablespoons olive oil
- Salt and freshly milled black pepper
- 1 head radicchio, shredded

Separate the egg whites from the yolks. Mince the whites and reserve. Put the yolks in a bowl and mash with a fork. Reserve.

In a large serving bowl, mash the tuna, mayonnaise, and lemon juice with a fork until well combined and creamy. Add the reserved egg whites, pickled vegetables, peas, capers, cocktail onions, carrot, celery, potato, olives, and olive oil and mix to combine. Season to taste with salt and pepper.

Serve on a bed of radicchio. Sprinkle with the egg yolks just before serving.

Libiamo ne' lieti calici,

Let us drink from the joyful goblets

Che la bellezza infiora;

That beauty decks with flowers;

E la fuggevol ora

And may the fleeting hour

S'inebrii a voluttà.

Become intoxicated with pleasure.

Libiam ne' dolci fremiti

Let us drink the sweet excitement

Che suscita l'amore,

That love arouses,

Poichè quell'occhio al core

Since her omnipotent glance

Onnipotente va.

Goes to the heart.

LA TRAVIATA

FOCACCIA CON ROSMARINO
Makes 2 focaccia, roughly 6 by 10 inches wide

I like to imagine that Friar Melitone is doling out this heavenly treat for the poor in *La Forza del Destino*.

I'm not a bread baker. I don't mean just that I don't bake bread for a living, I mean I don't usually bake bread. The breads I make just don't turn out as good as professionally baked ones. I'm sure it has to do with their industrial strength ovens or needing a white thumb or something! Bottom line: I mostly leave bread making to the professionals.

Maybe this confession isn't what you would expect in the introduction to a bread recipe, but I'm hoping my candor will win your confidence and that you'll believe me when I tell you to try this recipe. Follow these directions and you'll have a focaccia better-tasting than a professional's.

> 1 package active dry yeast, about ¼ ounce
>
> 3 tablespoons honey
>
> 2 cups all-purpose flour, plus more as needed
>
> 5 tablespoons extra-virgin olive oil
>
> 2 tablespoons fine salt
>
> 4 tablespoons fresh rosemary
>
> Semolina flour or coarse cornmeal, for dusting
>
> 1 tablespoon coarse sea salt

Combine the yeast, honey, and 1 cup warm water in a large bowl and let rest 10 minutes to activate the yeast. Add 1 cup of the flour, 2 tablespoons of the oil, and the fine salt and combine with a fork or electric beater.

Slowly add the remaining 1 cup flour until combined. Lightly flour your hands and knead the dough in the bowl, adding a bit more flour, if necessary, to keep the dough from sticking. Knead for about 5 minutes, until the dough feels elastic.

Place the dough in a lightly greased bowl. Allow it to rise, covered, in a warm, dry spot until doubled in size, about 1 hour.

Add 2 tablespoons of the rosemary, knead the dough again for a few minutes, then divide it in half. With the palm of your hand, press each section into a rectangle about 6 inches by 10 inches. Place the rectangles onto a baking pan liberally dusted with semolina flour or cornmeal.

Mix the remaining 2 tablespoons rosemary with 2 tablespoons of the oil in a small bowl and spread onto the focaccia. Press your fingertips repeatedly down into the dough to incorporate the herbs and oil.

Allow to rise for 30 to 40 minutes. Meanwhile, preheat the oven to 500°F

Bake the focaccia until golden, about 15 minutes. Drizzle with the remaining tablespoon of olive oil and sprinkle with coarse salt.

La Forza del Destino

Secondo Piatto

OSSO BUCCO CAN BE MADE THE DAY BEFORE YOUR DINNER PARTY. In fact, most of the recipes in this chapter can be made a day ahead. The only dish that requires last-minute attention is the risotto. But since risotto only requires stirring, you can easily carry on a lively conversation with guests while it cooks.

At my dinner parties, after the primi piatti—the soup and pasta courses—I suggest that guests move about. Some go off to chat in the living room, others stay at the table, and a few keep me company in the kitchen while I stir the risotto.

When we return to the table for the main course, I'll often swap places with my husband at the other end of the table. You'll be surprised what a nice lift it gives a dinner party when you reshuffle things that way. Everyone loves it, and it's a great way to keep the evening lively.

OSSO *NABUCCO*
Serves 4 to 6

Osso bucco, a traditional dish from Milan, should be in every cook's repertoire. It's elegant, homey, and perfect for entertaining because it can be made a day or two ahead.

To give the dish extra color, use a mix of green, yellow, and orange heirloom tomatoes as well as red. The gremolata topping, a blend of parsley, garlic, and lemon zest, imparts a distinctive aroma and flavor and is the hallmark of authentic osso bucco.

Ossobucco means "bones with holes." You'll understand this when you see your guests gobble everything on their plates, including the scrumptious bone marrow in the center. All that's left is bones with holes.

4 to 6 bone-in veal shanks, about 1½ inches thick, tied with kitchen string

Salt and freshly milled black pepper

All-purpose flour, for dredging

2 to 3 tablespoons extra-virgin olive oil

2 small carrots, finely minced

1 stalk celery, minced

1 large onion, minced

5 cloves garlic, finely minced

2 bay leaves

1 tablespoon dried marjoram

1½ cups white wine

¾ cup best-quality beef stock, plus more as needed

8 to 9 heirloom tomatoes, assorted colors, peeled, halved, and seeded

½ cup finely minced fresh parsley leaves

Zest of 2 lemons

1 to 2 anchovy fillets, finely mashed

Pinch of fresh rosemary leaves

Preheat the oven to 350°F.

Season both sides of the shanks with salt and pepper and dredge them in flour. Heat the oil in an ovenproof casserole over medium-high heat and sear the shanks until browned, 2 to 3 minutes per side. Remove the shanks and allow them to rest on a plate while you prepare the sauce.

Add the carrots, celery, and onion to the same casserole, reduce the heat to medium, and cook until the vegetables are tender, about 6 minutes.

Add about two-thirds of the minced garlic, the bay leaves, and the marjoram and sauté for about 1 minute. Add the wine and simmer for 2 to 3 minutes. Using a wooden spoon, scrape free the flavorful browned bits from the bottom of the casserole, incorporating them into the sauce. Add the stock and bring to a boil. Remove from the heat and pour the sauce into a separate bowl. Reserve.

Arrange the shanks in one layer in the casserole, and top with some of the reserved sauce and 4 of the tomato halves. Cover and bake. Cook for 2 hours, then add the rest of the tomatoes, and cook for another 30 minutes. Every 30 minutes during the 2-hour cooking period, turn the shanks, adding more stock, only if needed.

At this point, you can refrigerate the dish for 24 hours, if you like. Just before serving, reheat the shanks on the stovetop and continue with the instructions below.

Remove the shanks and tomatoes from the pan and reserve, covered, to keep them warm.

Place the casserole on the stovetop over a medium heat and stir in ¼ cup of the parsley, half the lemon zest, and the anchovy fillets. Stir the anchovy fillets into the sauce until they dissolve. Scrape all the pan solids so they combine with the liquid. Simmer the stock until it thickens slightly. Season to taste with salt and pepper.

Meanwhile, prepare the gremolata topping by mixing the remaining ¼ cup parsley, the remaining minced garlic, the rosemary, and the remaining lemon zest in a small bowl until well combined.

To serve, place a few spoonfuls of the sauce on a plate topped with one shank and three or four tomato sections. Top with more sauce and a generous scattering of gremolata.

OPERA NOTE

Enrico Caruso, who debuted at the Metropolitan Opera in 1903 in *Rigoletto*, performed there more times than the sum of all his other opera appearances elsewhere.

HERB RISOTTO
Serves 6

The aromatic herbs stirred into the dish after it's cooked produce a bright, colorful, and fragrant risotto. In Italy risotto is always a primo piatto, a first-course dish, served on its own. The single exception is that it is always served as a side dish for osso bucco.

The secret to making perfect risotto, with firm grains and no stickiness, is adding hot stock as the rice cooks. Another tip for great-tasting risotto is not to add salt until the very end, after the Parmesan cheese, which contains lots of its own salt.

- **4 to 5 cups best-quality chicken stock**
- **3 tablespoons extra-virgin olive oil**
- **1 large Vidalia or purple onion, minced**
- **1 pound Arborio rice, about 2¼ cups**
- **3 tablespoons unsalted butter, softened**
- **1½ cups assorted fresh herbs such as parsley, mint, rosemary, sage, and basil**
- **¾ cup grated Parmesan cheese**
- **Salt and freshly milled black pepper**

In a small saucepan over medium heat, bring the stock to a low boil.

Heat the oil in a large skillet over medium heat and sauté the onion until it is translucent, about 6 minutes.

Add the rice and, stirring constantly, sauté for about 3 minutes. Add 1 cup of the hot stock and stir until the stock is absorbed. Add more stock, ¼ cup at a time, stirring constantly, until the rice is tender, about 25 minutes.

Meanwhile, puree the butter and herbs in a food processor.

Remove the rice from the heat, stir in the butter-herb mixture and the Parmesan. Taste and only then season with salt and pepper, if needed.

Serve immediately.

Dolci

CITRUS HONEY PYRAMID
Serves 10 to 12

You're going to have so much fun with this dessert!

The dough is formed into little balls and fried. Don't worry, though—it isn't at all greasy! The balls puff up into perfect nibble-sized bites, which are then coated with a delicious citrus honey and stacked into a pyramid shape. A scatter of brown sugar around the base completes the look.

Guests break off pieces of the pyramid for a communal dessert that is as entertaining to eat as it is to make.

> 2½ cups all-purpose flour, plus more as needed
>
> 5 tablespoons granulated sugar
>
> 1½ teaspoons baking soda
>
> ¼ teaspoon salt
>
> 6 eggs
>
> 4 tablespoons (½ stick) unsalted butter, melted
>
> 3 tablespoons Cointreau or limoncella
>
> 1 tablespoon vanilla extract
>
> Zest of 1 lemon
>
> Zest of 1 orange
>
> Canola or walnut oil, for frying
>
> 12 ounces honey, about 1½ cups
>
> ¼ cup finely minced candied orange peel
>
> Brown sugar

In a large bowl, using an electric mixer, combine the flour, 3 tablespoons of the granulated sugar, baking soda, salt, 4 whole eggs, 2 yolks, butter, Cointreau, vanilla, and the zests until a dough forms. Refrigerate it for 20 minutes.

Take a small handful of the dough and roll it into a breadstick shape about ¾ inch in diameter. In a high-sided saucepan, heat 3 inches of oil over medium heat.

Cut the dough into hazelnut-sized sections about ½ inch thick, roll into balls, and fry them in the hot oil. They will puff up and turn a lovely golden color within seconds. Remove them from the skillet and place them onto a paper-towel-lined plate.

Repeat until all the remaining dough has been used.

In a medium saucepan, combine the honey, the remaining 2 tablespoons of granulated sugar, and the candied orange peel and bring to a boil. Remove from the heat and stir in the fried balls, one small batch at a time, until they are well coated in the honey mixture. Using a slotted spoon, remove the coated balls and arrange them in a square in a shallow bowl. That forms the base of the pyramid. Repeat with the remaining dough balls, decreasing the size of each successive layer to form a pyramid. When your structure is complete, pour any remaining honey and candied peel over the top.

Depending on the size of your serving bowl, you might have enough balls to make two pyramids.

Just before serving, scatter the brown sugar around the base of the pyramid so it looks like sand. The dessert is placed in the center of the table and guests help themselves to the balls with their fingers.

NOTE: If you prefer, you can bake the dough balls. Place the hazelnut-sized dough segments about 1 inch apart on a well-greased baking sheet and bake at 400°F for about 7 minutes. Turn the balls over and continue baking for another 6 to 7 minutes, or until light golden. They will not be as round or as nicely golden as the fried version, but the taste will be just as stupendous. You might like to try baking half the dough and frying half so that your pyramid has color gradations.

Aida

AMARETTO-RUM BALLS
Serves 10 to 12, makes about 40 balls

I like simple, no-bake, make-ahead desserts like these yummy chocolate balls. They're a snap to prepare but always get compliments. They also keep for weeks.

Stack the rum balls in a pyramid shape as an ode to *Aida*.

2 cups finely crushed almond biscotti

1/4 cup Amaretto or other almond liqueur

1/4 cup rum

1 cup finely crushed almonds, hazelnuts, or walnuts

1/2 cup confectioners' sugar

6 ounces best-quality bittersweet chocolate, melted

3 tablespoons light corn syrup

Maple sugar or brown sugar

In a bowl, thoroughly combine the biscotti with the Amaretto and rum. Then stir in the nuts, confectioners' sugar, chocolate, and corn syrup until well blended.

Using your hands, take tablespoon-sized portions and form them into balls about 3/4 inch in diameter.

Put the maple sugar into a bowl and roll each chocolate ball in the sugar until well coated. Serve or store in an airtight container for up to 3 weeks.

OPERA NOTE

Verdi composed *Aida*, an opera set in ancient Egypt, in 1871, while living in Milan. After that he took a fifteen-year opera hiatus, coming out of semiretirement with *Otello*.

Chapter Seven

English Pub Supper
with Gilbert & Sullivan

Twenty love-sick maidens we,
Love-sick all against our will.
Twenty years hence we shall be
Twenty love-sick maidens still.
Twenty love-sick maidens we,
And we die for love of thee.

PATIENCE

ONLY A COUNTRY THAT IS HOME TO DISHES NAMED Bubble and Squeak with Wow Wow Sauce and Toad-in-the-Hole could have produced two such whimsical and witty artists as W. S. Gilbert and Arthur Sullivan. English food may have wacky names, but it's delicious.

A beer tasting is a wonderful excuse to try all sorts of brews while sharing with your mates snippets of your favorite Gilbert and Sullivan operettas, or even Stephen Sondheim's London-based *Sweeney Todd*. This chapter offers lots of tips for a successful tasting event. Besides classic brews, try beer concoctions like Shandy with lemonade, or Beer Flip, a frothy egg-and-spices hot toddy.

Menu

PUB BREWS

Shandy

English Bishop

Tarantara Hot Toddy

Beer Flip

PUB FARE

Yum-Yum Oyster Stew with Apple Crisps

Mrs. Lovett's Meat Pies

Scotch Eggs

Queen's Navee Fish and Chips

Shepherd's Pie

Toad-in-the-Hole

Bubble and Squeak with Wow Wow Sauce

TEA TIME

Little Buttercup Scones with Assorted Preserves

Sally Lunn Cake

Foolproof Fool

PREVIOUS PAGES: *Patience*

Pub Brews

YOU CAN ORGANIZE A BEER TASTING IN ANY NUMBER OF WAYS. Select a single type of brew, such as ale, which varies in color from gold to dark ruby. For example, focus your tasting on the range of ales that the British call "bitters," which aren't really bitter at all, but have a light fruity taste. Another way to organize your tasting is to compare the brews of different countries.

For a first time tasting, however, I suggest offering a range of brews. Offer a few top-fermenting yeast ales like barley wine, bitter, porter, stout, and wheat beer and a few choices of bottom-fermentation lagers like bock, pilsner, and Oktoberfest.

Six to eight brews is a good number, no matter which style of tasting you do. It's enough variety but not so much as to overwhelm the palate. Plan on four ounces of each choice per person, or about one bottle of beer for every three guests. Start the tasting with the beers that are lightest in flavor, like wheat beer, and move on in steps to more intense beers such as bock and stout.

Much as when you taste wine, take a minute to notice the color of the beer and the head's thickness. Sniff before tasting. What do you smell? Fruits like apple and plum or earthy scents like hay and grass? Do you smell butter or caramel? Once you taste, think about the flavor and crispness or pleasant bitterness you're experiencing.

SHANDY
Serves 1

Beer and lemonade? Don't turn up your nose until you've tried it! The combination is crisp and tart and will keep your interest to the bottom of the glass. This is a drink you'll want to enjoy icy cold.

You can substitute lemon soda, ginger ale, or ginger beer for the lemonade.

> **Freshly squeezed juice of 2 lemons**
> **Sugar**
> **4 ounces pale or light ale, chilled**

Combine the lemon juice with about 8 ounces of cold water in a tall glass. Sweeten to taste with sugar and slowly add the ale.

Pour, oh, pour the pirate sherry

Fill, oh, fill the pirate glass.

And, to make us more than merry,

Let the pirate bumper pass.

THE PIRATES OF PENZANCE

ENGLISH BISHOP
Serves 4 to 6, makes 1 quart

This is a very old English recipe that was served when the vicar stopped by. Jonathan Swift even wrote a rhyme about it:

Fine orange well roasted, with wine in a cup,
They'll make a sweet bishop when gentle folks sup.

It might sound like a lot of work to roast an orange, but it's just a matter of wrapping it in aluminum foil and popping it into the oven. This drink is delicious.

- 12 whole cloves
- 1 navel orange
- 2 tablespoons sugar
- One 2-inch stick of cinnamon
- 2 tablespoons candied ginger, or 3 tablespoons grated fresh ginger
- Pinch of ground allspice
- 2 blades mace, optional
- One 750-ml bottle ruby port wine
- Freshly grated nutmeg

Preheat the oven to 450°F.

Stick the cloves into the orange, wrap it in a double layer of aluminum foil, and place it on a small baking pan. Bake the orange for 30 minutes. Remove the orange from the oven and raise the temperature to broil.

Open the foil and slice the orange in half. With the skin side up, put the orange halves under the broiler for a minute or two until dark golden. Reserve.

In a large saucepan bring 1 cup water to a boil with the sugar, cinnamon, ginger, allspice, and mace, if using. Simmer for 5 minutes. Add the roasted orange and any juice it released and the port and simmer until warm, about 5 minutes. Strain and serve hot in mugs with a sprinkle of nutmeg.

TARANTARA HOT TODDY
Serves 4

Wonderful on a dank winter evening. The warm spices and rum smell divine and taste bewitching. Just the sort of nightcap Major General Stanley could have used after his run-in with the pirates. Tarantara!

- 2 tablespoons brown sugar
- 6 ounces rum
- Pinch of ground allspice or cloves
- Pinch of freshly ground nutmeg
- 4 thin pats butter
- 4 cinnamon sticks

In a small saucepan, bring 1 cup water to a boil and stir in the brown sugar.

Remove from the heat and add the rum, allspice, and nutmeg. Pour into 4 mugs and top each with a pat of butter. Insert a cinnamon stick into each mug.

OPERA NOTE

Gilbert and Sullivan were a famously contentious pair. Their relationship began to decline in 1890 after what's come to be known as the "carpet quarrel." Their producer and partner, Richard D'Oyly Carte, sent them a bill for a carpet that was newly installed in the theater. Sullivan didn't particularly mind, but Gilbert was indignant at the invoice and at his partner's indifference.

This led Gilbert to a dizzying falling-out with his partners—financial squabbling with D'Oyly Carte and a suspended collaboration with Sullivan. The partnership eventually resumed, but relations remained cold.

The Pirates of Penzance

BEER FLIP
Serves 4 to 6, makes 1 quart

The "flip," a frothy beer drink mixed with eggs, has been popular in England since the Middle Ages. The eggs give the beer great body and taste. If you've never tried one, you're in for a surprising treat. Even people who don't like beer love flips.

The name comes from "flip irons," hot fireplace pokers, which used to be plunged into beer and egg concoctions to heat them.

> **6 eggs, separated**
> **½ cup orange juice**
> **2 tablespoons sugar**
> **½ teaspoon freshly grated nutmeg**
> **Pinch of cinnamon**
> **Pinch of allspice**
> **1 quart beer**

In a bowl whisk the egg yolks, orange juice, sugar, nutmeg, cinnamon, and allspice until well combined. In another bowl, using an electric mixer, beat the egg whites until stiff peaks form.

Heat the beer in a saucepan over medium heat until hot.

Remove the beer from the heat and whisk in the egg yolk mixture until very smooth. Whisk in the egg whites and pour back and forth once or twice between the saucepan and the bowl to develop a frothy head.

Serve immediately in mugs.

Pub Fare

YUM-YUM OYSTER STEW WITH APPLE CRISPS
Serves 4

Just like Gilbert and Sullivan's most famous heroine, the delectable but self-involved schoolgirl Yum-Yum, this oyster stew is creamy and sweet, but with a touch of tartness. A winning combination, especially when accompanied by a pint. Yum!

- ½ cup superfine sugar
- 1 Granny Smith apple, core removed with a corer, peel still on
- 1 large red onion, diced
- 2 tablespoons unsalted butter
- 1 cup white wine
- 12 small oysters, liquid reserved
- 1 cup half-and-half
- ½ teaspoon freshly ground nutmeg
- Salt
- Pink peppercorns, for serving

Preheat the oven to 200°F. Line a baking sheet with parchment paper and set aside.

Sprinkle the sugar on a plate. Using a very sharp knife or a mandoline, slice the apple into paper-thin rounds. Dredge the apple slices in the sugar until well coated. Place the slices on the prepared cookie sheet.

Bake for about 1 hour, turn the slices, and bake another hour, until the slices are a light golden color and quite crisp. Place the chips in a single layer on a wire rack to cool.

Meanwhile, sauté the onion and butter in a saucepan over medium heat for 10 minutes, until very soft. Add the wine and bring to a boil. Reduce to low heat, add the oysters and their liquid, and cook for about 4 minutes. Add the half-and-half, nutmeg, and salt to taste. Simmer for about 3 minutes until warm.

Ladle the stew into the serving bowl and top with a sprinkling of pink peppercorns and the apple crisps.

OPERA NOTE

W. S. Gilbert was so nervous on opening nights that he couldn't eat.

Sullivan stayed up working until seven in the morning on the day of the New York world premiere of *Pirates of Penzance*, fortified by a supper of oysters and champagne.

OPERA NOTE

W.S. Gilbert was kidnapped in Naples, Italy, when he was two years old. He was quickly ransomed and returned to his family, but the episode may well have left a lasting impression. Though wit and high humor prevail, kidnapping is sung about in *The Gondoliers* and in *Pirates of Penzance* (where the maids might have been kidnapped, had they not been so willing to "marry with impunity").

MRS. LOVETT'S MEAT PIES
Serves 8 to 10

These delicious meat pies are a snap to make, thanks to ready-made freezer-case puff pastry, which always bakes up light and golden. The combination of sweet dried fruits and aromatic spices mixed with ground meat makes these little turnovers an irresistible snack.

½ pound ground pork or beef

2 tablespoons pine nuts

6 dates, pitted and finely chopped

3 dried apricots, finely chopped

¼ teaspoon freshly ground nutmeg

2 tablespoons light brown sugar

2 tablespoons orange liqueur or orange juice

½ teaspoon salt

¼ teaspoon freshly milled black pepper

1 box frozen puff pastry, thawed

Flour, for rolling out the dough

1 large egg, beaten

Place the ground meat, pine nuts, dates, apricots, nutmeg, brown sugar, orange liqueur, salt, and pepper in a bowl and mix well. Refrigerate for at least 1 hour, so the flavors can mingle.

Preheat the oven to 350°F.

Roll out the puff pastry ⅛ inch thick on a floured work surface. Using a 3- to 4-inch round cookie-cutter, press out dough circles. Place 2 tablespoons of the meat mixture on each circle, fold in half, and pinch the edges to seal. Place the turnovers on a nonstick baking sheet and brush the tops with the egg.

Bake for 20 minutes, or until golden brown. Serve warm.

Is it really good?

Sir, it's too good, at least.

SWEENEY TODD

SCOTCH EGGS
Serves 6

Essentially an egg inside a meatball, Scotch Eggs is a pub staple. I also tried the recipe with small red potatoes in place of the eggs, and it was absolutely delicious. Yukon gold or blue new potatoes make a beautiful, if somewhat untraditional, center. You can try both; just substitute three potatoes for three of the hard-boiled eggs in this recipe.

Use any sort of ground meat you like for the outer layer—pork, beef, lamb, or sausage.

1½ cups dry bread crumbs

2 teaspoons ground mace

Salt and freshly milled black pepper

¾ pound ground pork or beef

3 tablespoons finely minced fresh parsley

3 tablespoons finely minced red onion

1 tablespoon fennel seeds

6 hard-boiled eggs, peeled

2 raw eggs, beaten

Vegetable oil, for frying

In a shallow dish, combine the bread crumbs, mace, and salt and pepper to taste. Reserve.

In a medium bowl, mix together the ground meat, parsley, onion, fennel, and salt and pepper to taste. Divide into 6 portions.

Take a portion of meat into your hand and flatten it. Place a hard-boiled egg in the middle of the meat portion. Mold the meat mixture around the egg. Dip the ball into the beaten eggs and then coat with the bread crumbs, pressing to be sure they adhere.

Repeat until all 6 Scotch Eggs are assembled.

Heat about 1 inch of vegetable oil in a skillet over medium-high heat and fry the eggs until golden brown on all sides. Transfer them to a paper-towel-lined plate to drain.

Serve at room temperature.

QUEEN'S NAVEE FISH AND CHIPS
Serves 4

The quintessential English snack, fish and chips, is made with a beer batter that's flavorful, light, and simple to make.

I don't bother peeling the potatoes. I like chips with the skin on for a color contrast. But no matter how you slice them, the key to authentic fish and chips is to serve the chips with good cider or malt vinegar and HP Sauce, a truly inspired alternative to the same old ketchup standby.

- 1 cup all-purpose flour
- 1/2 teaspoon baking soda
- Salt and freshly milled black pepper
- 1 cup beer or ale
- Vegetable oil, for frying
- 4 large russet potatoes, peeled and cut into long strips
- 1 to 1 1/2 pounds cod or haddock fillet, skins left on, cut into 2-inch-wide strips
- Cider or malt vinegar, for serving

In a shallow bowl, combine the flour, baking soda, and a generous portion of salt and pepper. Slowly add the beer, stirring until very smooth. Let the batter rest while you make the chips.

Heat about 1 inch of oil in a large skillet over medium-high heat. Add the potatoes and fry until golden. Drain on a paper-towel-lined plate to remove any excess oil and season with salt while they're still hot.

Season the fish with salt and pepper. Dredge in the batter. In the same skillet that you used for the chips, fry the fish over medium-high heat until golden on each side. Add more oil, if needed.

Drain the fish on a paper-towel-lined plate to remove any excess oil.

Serve the chips and fish in a parchment paper cone with a bottle of vinegar on the side.

Now give three cheers,

I'll lead the way

Hurrah! Hurrah!

Hurray! Hurray! Hurray!

I am the monarch of the sea,

The ruler of the Queen's Navee,

Whose praise Great Britain loudly

chants.

HMS PINAFORE

England's Secret Ingredient

HP Sauce, a store-bought condiment made with malt vinegar, fruit, and spices, is the secret ingredient with fish and chips. Produced in Birmingham, England, but available in the States at specialty grocers or online, this sauce is a spicy-sweet Brit favorite. (See page 210 for sources.)

HP is fantastic with fish and chips, but you'll find yourself using it with lots of other foods as well. Try it in soups and stews or on a burger.

SHEPHERD'S PIE
Serves 6

Everyone loves shepherd's pie, the ultimate English pub comfort food.

Shepherd's pie, essentially stew topped with mashed potatoes, is traditionally made with Sunday supper's leftover roast lamb. Instead of using leftovers though, I start with uncooked meat cubes. It's just as easy but makes a more flavorful stew.

- 3 tablespoons olive oil
- 1 large Vidalia onion, chopped
- 1 1/2 pounds lamb or beef, cut into 1/2-inch cubes
- Salt and freshly milled black pepper
- All-purpose flour, for dredging
- 3 cloves garlic
- 3/4 pound assorted sliced mushrooms
- 1 cup white wine
- 1/2 cup best-quality chicken or beef stock
- 2 tablespoons tomato paste
- 3 tablespoons fresh thyme, or 1 1/2 teaspoons dried
- 3 tablespoons fresh tarragon, or 1 teaspoon dried
- 4 medium russet potatoes
- 4 tablespoons (1/2 stick) unsalted butter
- 3/4 cup whole milk
- Freshly grated nutmeg
- 2 to 3 tablespoons grated Cheddar cheese

Heat the oil in a medium-sized ovenproof casserole over medium heat and sauté the onion until golden, about 10 minutes.

Season the lamb with salt and pepper and dredge it in flour. Add the meat to the pan and cook until browned. Add the garlic and mushrooms and sauté for another minute until softened.

Stir in the wine and, using a wooden spoon, scrape the bottom of the casserole to loosen any bits of meat. Add the stock, tomato paste, thyme, and tarragon. Simmer over low heat, covered, for about 40 minutes. Season to taste with salt and pepper.

Meanwhile, boil the potatoes until soft. Peel and mash them in a bowl with the butter and milk. Season to taste with salt, pepper, and nutmeg.

Preheat the oven to 350°F.

Top the lamb stew with the mashed potatoes. Bake the casserole, uncovered, for about 30 minutes. Set the oven to broil, sprinkle the cheese over the pie, and broil until golden, about 3 minutes.

NOTE: I cut corners wherever I can, as long as it doesn't compromise the flavor or look of a dish. Everyone I know who makes shepherd's pie makes the stew part in one pot and then transfers it to a pie pan or casserole. That makes two pots to wash: the one you made the stew in and the one you baked the stew in.

I use an ovenproof casserole to make the stew and then use the same casserole to bake it. Casseroles go from oven to table, so why not from stovetop to oven to table? One less pot to wash!

Or we have some shepherd's pie peppered

With actual shepherd

On top.

SWEENEY TODD

TOAD-IN-THE-HOLE
Serves 6

Toad-in-the-Hole, a delicious popover featuring a crispy "toad" breakfast sausage peeking out, is a nineteenth-century classic still popular today.

The easy-to-make Yorkshire pudding batter rises wonderfully high and bakes to a glorious golden brown. The inside of the popover is flaky and oh-so-light.

The secret to its crispy outside and flaky inside is to preheat the muffin pan until piping hot before you pour in the batter. The popovers are also great without the "toads."

- **2 eggs**
- **$3/4$ cup whole milk**
- **$1/4$ teaspoon salt**
- **$1/4$ teaspoon freshly milled black pepper**
- **$3/4$ cup all-purpose flour**
- **6 pork or beef breakfast sausages**

Preheat the oven to 450°F. Put a muffin tray into the oven to heat.

Combine the eggs, milk, salt, and pepper in a medium bowl and, using an electric blender or whisk, beat the mixture until frothy. Slowly beat in the flour until the batter is smooth and bubbles have formed. Cover with plastic wrap and refrigerate while you fry the sausage.

In a small skillet, fry the sausages until they are golden and cooked through. Take the muffin tin out of the oven and, while it's still hot, put a sausage and a little of the pan grease into each of 6 muffin sections. Whisk the batter again and pour it over the sausages.

Bake for about 10 minutes and without opening the oven door reduce the heat to 350°F. Bake for about 15 minutes more, until golden.

Serve immediately.

By the mystic regulation
Of our dark Association,
Ere you open conversation
With another kindred soul,
You must eat a sausageroll!
You must eat a sausageroll!

THE GRAND DUKE

OPERA NOTE

W. S. Gilbert had a complicated relationship
with his popularity. Though he was
proud of his librettos, he sometimes
derided them in private letters.
In undertaking *The Yeomen of the Guard*,
the duo's most serious opera,
Gilbert was moved to write to his friend
Mary Leslie, "I don't want you to
judge me by the Jack Pudding
nonsense with which my name is now
associated" (January 6, 1888).

Then a sentimental passion

Of a vegetable fashion

Must excite your languid spleen,

An attachment à la Plato

For a bashful young potato,

Or a not too French French bean!

PATIENCE

BUBBLE AND SQUEAK WITH WOW WOW SAUCE
Serves 4

What a ridiculous name for what is essentially leftover mashed potatoes and cabbage. I would never have tried it, except that I was curious about two things.

First, I wanted to know if the origin of the name is true. The 1800s cookbooks with this recipe suggest that the dish is noisy while it's cooking. Many cookbooks even included little songs, "When 'midst the frying Pan, in accents savage, this Beef so surly, quarrels with the Cabbage." So, I wanted to find out if it really does bubble and squeak.

Second, I wanted to understand why everyone sighs so contentedly and smiles so lovingly when I ask about the dish.

I made a huge batch and invited a dozen non-British friends to try it. I learned both answers. One, yes, it does indeed make a ridiculously riotous ruckus in the pan. The moisture in the cabbage creates steam under the blanket of mashed potatoes, squeaking frantically while escaping through the bubbling potatoes.

Two, even non-Brits loved this dish. The whole is truly greater than the parts. People who hate cabbage loved it. People who hate vegetables loved it. Fussy eaters who usually hate everything loved it.

One of the best parts is the wow wow sauce. Its ridiculous name supposedly originated in the early nineteenth century because anyone tasting the dish exclaimed, "Wow, oh wow!" I suspect that the author of the dish invented the name too. But what's in a name? The taste's the thing! Simple to prepare with pantry staples, wow wow has a lush creaminess with hints of port, a little tang of Worcestershire, and the bite of English mustard. It's a pretty caramel brown and goes wonderfully with bubble and squeak and just about any broiled or grilled meat or veggie. This is a sauce you'll make over and over.

A great way to use leftover mashed potatoes and get a laugh at the same time.

2 tablespoons unsalted butter

2 tablespoons all-purpose flour

1 cup best-quality chicken, beef, or vegetable stock

3 tablespoons port or sherry

2 tablespoons white wine vinegar

1 tablespoon Worcestershire sauce

2 tablespoons Coleman's prepared mustard

2 tablespoons finely minced fresh parsley, plus more
for garnish

Salt and freshly milled black pepper

1 small cabbage, about 4 cups cubed

2 tablespoons olive oil

½ pound bacon, diced

1 large Vidalia onion, chopped

2 to 3 cups leftover mashed potatoes

To make the wow wow sauce, melt the butter in a medium saucepan over low heat. Stir in the flour until smooth and then slowly add the stock, stirring constantly until smooth.

Add the, port, vinegar, Worcestershire sauce, and mustard and simmer for 10 minutes. Remove from the heat and stir in the parsley. Season to taste with salt and pepper. Transfer the sauce to a small serving bowl, but don't rinse out the saucepan. Use it to cook the cabbage.

Add 1½ cups water to the saucepan and bring to a boil. Add the cabbage and a pinch of salt. Cover and cook until tender. Drain and reserve.

Heat the oil in a large skillet over medium heat and cook the bacon with the onions until browned. Stir in the mashed potatoes until well combined and then stir in the cabbage. Press down the mashed potato–cabbage mixture with a spatula or wooden spoon. Season the top of the bubble and squeak with salt and pepper and allow to cook in the pan until the underside is golden (about 5 minutes). Carefully turn the mixture over in sections. Season the top with salt and pepper and cook until the underside is golden.

Serve topped with the wow wow sauce and a sprinkle of parsley.

The Pirates of Penzance

OPERA NOTE

According to legend, W. S. Gilbert once scolded an actor for not knowing his lines. The actor argued back saying, "See here, sir! I will not be bullied. I know my lines." To which Gilbert quickly retorted, "Possibly, but you don't know mine!"

Tea Time

LONDON OWES ONE OF ITS FAVORITE HOT SPOTS FOR AFTERNOON TEA, the Savoy Hotel, to the success of Gilbert & Sullivan. Eight years after he opened the Savoy Theatre, Richard D'Oyly Carte, the duo's partner, built the hotel with the considerable profits from Gilbert & Sullivan's operettas.

LITTLE BUTTERCUP SCONES WITH ASSORTED PRESERVES
Serves 6

This dough is very forgiving, so it's great for kids and novice cooks. You don't have to wait for anything to rise and you barely have to knead the dough. Just mix a few pantry basics with butter and milk, and in twelve minutes you have warm, flaky, melt-in-your-mouth scones.

You can customize the scones by adding chocolate chips, bacon bits, cheese, or dried fruit. Try them plain, too, so you can serve them with preserves, lemon curd, honey, or clotted cream.

2 cups all-purpose flour

1 tablespoon sugar

1/4 teaspoon salt

4 tablespoons (1/2 stick) unsalted butter, cold, cut into small pieces

1/2 cup whole milk

1/2 teaspoon baking soda

Assorted preserves, for serving

English clotted cream, for serving

Preheat the oven to 375°F and line a baking sheet with parchment.

In a large bowl, stir together the flour, sugar, and salt. Mix the butter into the dry ingredients with a fork or with your fingers until it is broken down into pea-sized lumps.

Stir in the milk and baking soda, mixing until the dough begins to come together. Turn it out onto a floured work surface and knead it very briefly. Do not overwork the dough. It is supposed to be a little dry.

Pat the dough out into a 6-inch circle and cut it into 6 pie-shaped wedges. Transfer the scones to the baking sheet and bake until light golden, 12 to 14 minutes.

Serve warm with preserves and clotted cream.

*I've treacle and toffee, I've tea and
I've coffee,*

Soft tommy and succulent chops;

*I've chickens and conies, and pretty
polonies,*

And excellent peppermint drops.

*Then buy of your Buttercup—dear
Little Buttercup;*

Sailors should never be shy;

*So, buy of your Buttercup—poor
Little Buttercup;*

Come, of your Buttercup buy!

HMS PINAFORE

SALLY LUNN CAKE
Serves 10

Named after an eighteenth-century baker, Sally Lunn is one of my favorite cakes. Actually, it's more like moist, dense white bread than cake because there's no sugar at all in the recipe. It's a perfect teatime treat that gets its sweetness from what you put on it. Sally Lunn is like a little black dress—you can dress it up or down with accessories, in this case of jam, jellies, ice cream, or whipped cream.

I should mention another great aspect of the cake. It's easy to make and doesn't create a mess. Just mix all the ingredients in one bowl and you're done.

- 2 packages active dry yeast, about ½ ounce total
- 2 cups whole milk, warm
- 4 cups all-purpose flour
- 3 large eggs, beaten
- 2 tablespoons unsalted butter, melted, plus more for serving
- 1 teaspoon salt
- Assorted jams, for serving
- Whipped cream, for serving

Generously butter a 12-cup Bundt pan and set aside.

In a large bowl, sprinkle the yeast over the warm milk and stir to dissolve. Let rest for 10 minutes to active the yeast.

Slowly add the flour, mixing well after each addition. Then add the eggs, butter, and salt and stir briskly until the batter is smooth. Pour the batter into the prepared Bundt pan, cover, and allow to rise at room temperature for 1 hour.

Preheat the oven to 400°F.

Bake the cake until light golden, about 20 minutes. Allow it to cool for 5 minutes in the pan, then invert onto a rack and cool completely before cutting.

Serve with assorted jams, butter, and whipped cream.

FOOLPROOF FOOL
Serves 4

Fool is a classic English dessert of whipped cream with sweetened gooseberries, but you can use any fruit you like.

- 2 pints gooseberries, washed and any stems removed
- 3 tablespoons granulated sugar
- 2 tablespoons unsalted butter
- Pinch of freshly ground nutmeg
- 1 cup heavy cream
- Raw or granulated brown sugar

Place the gooseberries, granulated sugar, butter, and nutmeg in a small saucepan and simmer over low heat for 10 minutes. Mash with a fork and press through a strainer to remove the seeds and skins. Cool to room temperature and refrigerate, covered, until cold.

Whip the cream until soft peaks form.

To serve, divide the whipped cream between 4 small serving glasses and gently stir in the gooseberry mixture. Top with a sprinkle of brown sugar.

Now to the banquet we press;

Now for the eggs and the ham;

Now for the mustard and cress,

Now for the strawberry jam!

Now for the tea of our host,

Now for the rollicking bun,

Now for the muffin and toast,

Now for the gay Sally Lunn!

THE SORCERER

Chapter Eight

Viva il vino spumeggiante

Here's to sparkling wine

Nel bicchiere scintillante,

In glittering glasses,

Come il riso dell'amante

Wine that awakens joy

Mite infonde il giubilo!

Like a lover's laughter.

Viva il vino ch'è sincero

Here's to wine that is pure,

Che ci allieta ogni pensiero,

That awakens the heart to rapture,

E che affoga l'umor nero,

And in gay abandon

Nell'ebbrezza tenera.

Drowns each somber thought.

CAVALLERIA RUSTICANA

Sicilian Picnic

CAVALLERIA RUSTICANA AND PAGLIACCI ARE EXAMPLES OF *VERISMO*, the late-1800s Italian movement toward realism in literature, art, and music, with a particular fascination with everyday life, especially of the lower classes in southern Italy.

This menu celebrates verismo with a selection of rustic Sicilian and Neapolitan dishes. Traditionally served cold or at room temperature, they are perfect for dining al fresco. You'll enjoy a sampling of classic Sicilian starters like Mamma Lucia's Sweet and Tangy Eggplant Caponata, a vegetarian delight of smoky eggplant, crunchy celery, and salty olives in a wonderfully sweet and tart tomato sauce. You'll love Hearty Farro Seafood Salad, a nutty-sweet whole grain in a light vinaigrette loaded with your favorite seafood. Sicilian Stuffed Beef Roll will steal the show at your picnic. It is one of the most beautiful and delicious dishes in Sicilian cuisine. End your feast with a traditional southern Italian pastry, Neapolitan Rum Baba Cake, a foolproof recipe that always bakes up perfectly. Or offer Nedda's Amaretti Roasted Peaches, filled with liqueur-soaked almond cookies: light yet satisfying enough for the most demanding sweet tooth. *Alla fortuna vostra! A voi tutti salute!*

Menu

APPETIZERS

Mamma Lucia's Sweet and Tangy Eggplant Caponata
Orange and Fennel Salad with Mint Vinaigrette
Hearty Farro Seafood Salad

MAIN COURSE

Sicilian Stuffed Beef Roll
Roasted Potato Salad with Basil and Marsala
Tricolor Sweet Peppers with Caramelized Onions
Cardoons with Lemony Dipping Sauce

DESSERT

Neapolitan Rum Baba Cake
Nedda's Amaretti Roasted Peaches

PREVIOUS PAGES: *Cavalleria Rusticana*

Appetizers

S ERVE S ICILIAN WINE WITH YOUR AL FRESCO MEAL. My favorites are Mamertino, Marsala, and Eloro.

MAMMA LUCIA'S SWEET AND TANGY EGGPLANT CAPONATA
Serves 6 to 8

Caponata, Sicilian eggplant antipasto, is one of those dishes we tend to take for granted. You know what it tastes like, you've had it before, and you can buy it ready-made in jars. So why bother making it?

Homemade caponata, prepared even by inexperienced cooks, is vastly better. At home you'll use only best-quality balsamic vinegar and olive oil. You'll add some of the celery at the very end of cooking so the dish has a nice crunch. You'll adjust the sweetness and tang, adding a pinch more sugar or splash of vinegar, to suit your own taste buds. You'll see. This caponata will be better than any from a restaurant, deli, or jar.

- 2 medium eggplants, skin on, cut into 1-inch pieces
- Kosher salt
- ½ cup extra-virgin olive oil, plus more as needed
- 2 large Vidalia onions, thinly sliced
- 5 to 6 stalks celery, cut into 1-inch pieces
- 4 cloves garlic, minced
- 1¼ cup tomato puree
- 1 cup pitted green Sicilian olives
- ½ cup balsamic vinegar, plus more as needed
- ½ cup capers, drained
- 2 tablespoons sugar, plus more as needed
- Salt and freshly milled black pepper
- 2 tablespoons pine nuts or sliced almonds, toasted, for garnish
- Minced fresh parsley, for garnish
- Crusty Italian bread, for serving

Sprinkle the eggplant cubes with the kosher salt and place them in a colander. Set the colander in the sink and allow the eggplant to drain for 30 minutes. Pat with paper towels to remove the excess moisture.

Heat ¼ cup of the oil in a large nonstick skillet over medium-high heat. Cook the eggplant in batches so the cubes fry without crowding. Fry each batch until golden brown on all sides, about 5 minutes per batch. Remove the eggplant with a slotted spoon and transfer to a paper-towel-lined plate to drain. Repeat with the remaining eggplant, adding more oil to the pan as necessary.

In the same pan, heat the remaining ¼ cup oil over medium-low heat. Add the onions and all but about 8 pieces of the celery and sauté, stirring occasionally, for about 10 minutes, until the onion is golden. Add the garlic and continue cooking until softened, about 2 minute. Stir in the tomato puree, olives, vinegar, capers, and sugar and simmer for about 10 minutes. Stir in the reserved eggplant and reserved celery pieces and simmer for about 5 minutes. Season to taste with salt and pepper and more sugar or vinegar, if needed.

Serve at room temperature topped with the pine nuts and parsley. Serve with slices of bread on the side.

ORANGE AND FENNEL SALAD WITH MINT VINAIGRETTE
Serves 4

Sweet oranges, licoricelike fennel, and red onions, at first read, may sound like a mismatched medley of ingredients. But after one bite you'll know why this trio has been a Sicilian classic for centuries.

Use small mason jars to prepare and store salad dressing. There's no whisk or bowl to clean, and the jars make handy containers for transporting and storing the dressing.

- 1/4 cup fresh mint leaves, plus more for garnish
- 3 tablespoons white wine vinegar
- 1 tablespoon honey
- 1/4 cup extra-virgin olive oil
- Salt and freshly milled black pepper
- 1 small red onion, sliced into very thin circles
- 1 fennel bulb, very thinly sliced, plus fronds for garnish
- 2 navel or blood oranges peeled and thinly sliced
- Black olives, for garnish, optional

For the vinaigrette, pulse the mint, vinegar, and honey together in a food processor until well combined. Slowly add the oil and pulse until well blended. Season to taste with salt and pepper.

Toss the vinaigrette with the onion rings and allow them to rest for 5 to 10 minutes, to soften the flavor.

To serve, arrange the fennel and oranges on a serving platter and top with the onions and vinaigrette. Garnish with fennel fronds and olives, if using.

HEARTY FARRO SEAFOOD SALAD
Serves 6 to 8

Have you tasted farro yet? It's a rustic whole grain that looks like a cross between chubby brown rice and barley. Farro, also called spelt, has been popular in Italy since ancient Roman times. It has a nutty flavor and high protein content, and is amazingly versatile. It can be used as stuffing for poultry or as a substitute for rice, couscous, or pasta. This seafood-rich farro dish is a popular Italian beach lunch.

Farro doesn't become soggy, making it perfect for dining al fresco or when you need to make a dish in advance. It's a not-to-be-missed delicacy.

- 1 pound farro
- 2 quarts best-quality chicken or vegetable stock
- 1 small red onion, finely minced
- 2 cloves garlic, finely minced
- 1/4 cup extra-virgin olive oil
- 2 tablespoons balsamic or red wine vinegar
- Freshly squeezed juice of 1 lemon
- 1 pint cherry tomatoes, cut in half
- 1/2 cup oil-cured pitted black olives, chopped
- 2 tablespoons capers, drained
- 1/4 cup minced fresh parsley
- 1/4 cup minced fresh basil
- 1/4 cup minced fresh mint
- 1 pound assorted cooked seafood such as tiny shrimp, diced lobster, mussels, clams, and flaked tuna packed in oil
- Salt and freshly milled black pepper
- Lemon wedges, for garnish

Put the farro into a bowl and cover it with cold water. Soak for 30 minutes and drain. In a large saucepan, bring the farro and stock to a boil over high heat. Reduce the heat to low and simmer, uncovered, for about 30 minutes, until tender.

Drain and transfer the hot farro to a serving bowl and immediately toss it with the onion, garlic, olive oil, and vinegar until well combined. Allow to cool and add the lemon juice, tomatoes, olives, capers, and herbs.

Gently stir in the seafood and season to taste with salt and pepper. Serve with lemon wedges.

Main Course

THIS RECIPE, LIKE ALL RECIPES FOR MEAT LOAF, MEATBALLS, AND BURGERS, calls for you to season the raw meat with salt and pepper to taste. But how do you do that short of having a little predinner steak tartare? How do you season something raw "to taste"?

If you're a professional cook, you just know. But the rest of us can season it lightly and then cook a little pinch in a small frying pan. That way we can sample it cooked and adjust the seasonings.

SICILIAN STUFFED BEEF ROLL
Serves 6 to 8

Please know that I've tried to limit myself to saying this only once per chapter, but this is really, truly a dish you absolutely must try. *Farsumagru* is like a jelly roll with tender steak outside and assorted Italian cold cuts, cheeses, seasoned ground meat, and boiled eggs inside.

The name, *farsumagru*, is Sicilian dialect for the Italian *falso magro*, meaning "false lean." It probably comes from the fact that, although the outside looks lean and even meager, the inside is decadently rich.

> 5 large eggs
>
> 3/4 pound ground beef or pork or a combination
>
> 1 large red onion, finely minced
>
> 2 to 3 cloves garlic, finely minced
>
> 6 ounces caciocavallo, Asiago, or pecorino cheese, coarsely grated
>
> 1/2 cup minced fresh parsley
>
> 2 tablespoons fresh thyme, plus sprigs as garnish
>
> Salt and freshly milled black pepper
>
> 1 1/2-pound round or flank steak, butterflied and pounded
>
> 4 to 6 thin slices mortadella or ham
>
> 6 to 8 thin slices sopressata or other salami
>
> 3 tablespoons olive oil, plus more as needed
>
> 1 cup red wine
>
> 2 bay leaves

Hard-boil 4 of the eggs. Peel them and cut off and discard the pointy white tips until you reach the yolk. Reserve.

In a bowl combine the raw egg, ground meat, onion, garlic, cheese, parsley, and thyme until well blended. Season to taste with salt and pepper. Reserve.

Place the steak on a cutting board or work surface and season both sides with salt and pepper. Top with one layer of mortadella and one layer of salami. Spread the ground meat mixture onto three quarters of the steak, pressing it down with a fork or wooden spoon. Line up the hard-boiled eggs, end to end, in the center of the ground meat mixture.

Starting at the ground meat end, roll the beef tightly and tie it with kitchen string.

In a heavy sauté or casserole pan large enough to contain the meat roll, heat the oil over high heat. Add the meat roll and brown it on all sides. Reduce the heat to low, pour the wine over the meat and add the bay leaves. Cover and simmer on low for about 50 minutes, turning the meat every 15 minutes so that it cooks evenly.

Allow to cool to room temperature, covered, in the pan, before slicing.

Serve sliced, topped with pan juices, and garnished with sprigs of thyme.

ROASTED POTATO SALAD WITH BASIL AND MARSALA
Serves 4

The secret to this extraordinary dish is to roast the potatoes in a hot oven until they're almost charred and then toss them in Marsala while they're still piping hot. This produces a nice double flavor, the smokiness of roasting and the sweet tang of Marsala.

The simple basil puree with oil and vinegar smells so tantalizing that you know even before the first bite that it's delicious.

> 8 to 10 small new potatoes
> 4 tablespoons olive oil
> ⅓ cup Marsala
> 10 to 12 large basil leaves, plus more for garnish
> 1 tablespoon aged balsamic vinegar
> Salt and freshly milled black pepper

Preheat the oven to 500°F.

Toss the potatoes with 2 tablespoons of the oil and bake on a baking sheet for about 20 minutes, or until tender. Cut the potatoes in half, transfer them to a serving bowl, and immediately toss with the Marsala.

In a small food processor or blender, puree the remaining 2 tablespoons oil, the basil, and vinegar until well combined. Toss the potatoes with the basil mixture and season to taste with salt and pepper.

Serve at room temperature garnished with slivers of basil leaves.

OPERA NOTE

Ruggero Leoncavallo was sued for plagiarism by Catulle Mendès after the premiere of *Pagliacci*. Mendès claimed Leoncavallo had taken the plot from his *La Femme du Tabarin* (1887). Leoncavallo argued that he based the opera not on anyone else's work, but on a murder that had occurred in Montalto, a village in Calabria. He even maintained that his own father was the presiding judge on the case.

TRICOLOR SWEET PEPPERS WITH CARAMELIZED ONIONS
Serves 4

This pretty red, yellow, and green sweet pepper dish is a southern Italian treasure. The slow-cooked onions caramelize to become candy-sweet and are balanced by the tang of red wine vinegar and oregano.

Delicious hot or cold, this dish travels well, making it an ideal picnic food.

1 large Vidalia or purple onion, sliced

4 tablespoons olive oil, plus more as needed

2 to 3 cloves garlic

1 red bell pepper, sliced

1 green bell pepper, sliced

1 yellow bell pepper, sliced

1 plum tomato, diced

2 tablespoons aged balsamic vinegar, plus more as needed

2 tablespoons fresh oregano, plus more for garnish

Salt and freshly milled black pepper

2 tablespoons minced fresh parsley, for garnish

In a large sauté pan, cook the onion in 2 tablespoons of the oil over medium heat for 10 minutes, until golden. Add the garlic and sauté another minute.

Add the peppers, tomato, vinegar, and oregano and cover. Cook until the peppers are tender, about 10 minutes.

Allow to come to room temperature and then season to taste with salt and pepper. Add an additional splash of oil or vinegar, if needed.

Serve topped with the parsley and garnished with oregano.

CARDOONS WITH LEMONY DIPPING SAUCE
Serves 4

A cardoon looks like gigantic prehistoric celery and tastes like the best artichoke heart you've ever eaten. It is by far my favorite vegetable. You can find it in natural food stores and specialty or gourmet grocery stores.

The classic Italian anchovy-accented lemon dipping sauce called *bagna cauda* delightfully enhances the cardoon's rich flavor. Bagna cauda is also wonderful with crudités.

Salt

4 cardoon ribs

1 egg

Dry bread crumbs

Freshly milled black pepper

Olive oil for frying, plus 3 tablespoons

1 clove garlic, minced

Freshly squeezed juice of 1/2 lemon

1/2 teaspoon dried marjoram

5 oil-packed anchovy fillets

2 tablespoons chopped fresh parsley

Bring a saucepan of salted water to a rapid boil. Wash the cardoons and strip away the fibers. Cut them into 3-inch lengths and put them into the boiling water. Cook until tender, about 3 minutes. Drain and allow to cool.

Beat the egg in a shallow bowl. Put the bread crumbs on a plate and season with salt and pepper. Dip the cardoon sections into the egg and dredge the bread crumbs.

Heat 1/2 inch oil in a skillet over medium-high heat. Fry the breaded cardoons in the oil until golden on both sides, about 4 minutes. Transfer them to a paper-towel-lined plate to absorb the excess oil. Reserve.

Heat 3 tablespoons of the oil in a small saucepan over medium heat. Add the garlic and cook until softened, 2 to 3 minutes. Stir in the lemon juice and marjoram and season to taste with salt and pepper. Return to a simmer and add the anchovies. Cook briefly until the anchovies dissolve, about 1 minute. Remove from the heat and stir in the parsley.

Serve the warm sauce with the cardoons.

Dessert

NAPLES, THE BIRTHPLACE OF RUGGERO LEONCAVALLO, is home to dozens of delectable desserts like sfogliatelle and spumoni.

NEAPOLITAN RUM BABA CAKE
Serves 8 to 10

One of my all-time favorite Neapolitan desserts, in fact one of my favorite desserts from anywhere, is rum baba—a rich brioche cake soaked in fruit and rum syrup. My version uses seductively fragrant passion fruit juice, sold in almost all health food stores. Instead of making individual babas, which require special baking gear, I make it into a large cake using an ordinary Bundt pan.

What I especially like about the recipe (besides that it's easy and delicious) is how versatile it is. Instead of the passion fruit and rum syrup, for variety you might like to try a slice topped with chocolate sauce, maple syrup, or a splash of your favorite liqueur. The variations are endless.

Without the syrup the brioche cake, which isn't too sweet, makes fabulous breakfast bread. Or use it to make a traditional Sicilian ice cream sandwich. Serve hazelnut ice cream book-ended by slices of the brioche, topped with a dollop of thick whipped cream.

- **2 packages active dry yeast, about ½ ounce total**
- **½ cup whole milk, warm**
- **3¼ cups sugar**
- **4 large eggs**
- **½ cup (1 stick) unsalted butter, melted, plus more, unmelted, for the pan**
- **1¾ cups all-purpose flour, plus more for the pan**
- **Zest of 1 orange**
- **¼ teaspoon salt**
- **1½ cups passion fruit or apricot juice**
- **Zest of 1 lemon**
- **¼ to ½ cup dark rum**
- **Whipped cream, for serving**

In a large bowl, combine the yeast, milk, and ¼ cup of the sugar. Let rest for about 5 minutes to activate the yeast. Using an electric hand mixer, blend in 3 of the eggs, 1 yolk, and melted butter, mixing until smooth. Slowly mix in the flour, a little at a time, until combined. Stir in the orange zest and salt. Allow to rest, lightly covered with plastic wrap, until the dough doubles in volume, about 45 minutes.

Meanwhile, preheat the oven to 375°F and lightly butter and flour a Bundt pan. In a medium saucepan, bring the fruit juice, the remaining 3 cups of sugar, and lemon zest to a boil. Reduce the heat and simmer until thickened, about 20 minutes. Stir in the rum to taste and reserve.

Transfer the dough to the Bundt pan and allow to rise for about 20 minutes. Bake until golden, about 20 minutes.

Remove the cake from the oven and allow it to cool just enough to transfer to a serving platter. Slowly, in drops, pour the rum syrup over the cake until it is completely absorbed.

Serve the cake at room temperature with a dollop of whipped cream.

OPERA NOTE

Pietro Mascagni, the creator of *Cavalleria Rusticana*, came from a family of professional bakers. His parents wanted him to enter the family trade and only reluctantly allowed him to study music instead.

NEDDA'S AMARETTI ROASTED PEACHES
Serves 4

You wouldn't think that anyone could improve on the taste of peaches, but the Italians did.

Filled with amaretti, those crisp little Italian almond cookies, and a splash of Amaretto, the peaches are then slow-roasted. The melding of the almondy flavors releases all the fruit's sweet potential.

Quick to assemble, light tasting, but oh-so-satisfying. Serve with a glass of Sicilian dessert wine like Moscato di Siracusa.

> 5 large peaches
>
> 12 amaretti, about 3 ounces
>
> 1/3 cup Amaretto or other almond liqueur, or Marsala wine, plus more as needed
>
> 1 large egg yolk
>
> 1/4 cup granulated sugar
>
> 4 tablespoons sliced almonds
>
> 2 tablespoons unsalted butter, plus more for the pan
>
> Confectioners' sugar, for serving

Preheat the oven to 350°F. Generously butter a baking pan. Reserve.

Cut the peaches in half and discard the pits. Using a grapefruit spoon or melon baller, scoop out the centers of 8 of the peach halves. Reserve the pulp.

Combine the pulp with the 2 remaining peach halves in a food processor or blender and pulse until smooth. Add the amaretti, liqueur, egg yolk, and granulated sugar and pulse until well combined. If the mixture is dry, add more liqueur.

Fill each peach half with the amaretti mixture. Top with sliced almonds and a very thin pat of butter. Arrange the halves onto the baking pan and bake for 30 minutes, until golden.

Serve at room temperature, topped with a sprinkle of confectioners' sugar.

Richard Tucker in _Pagliacci_

Vesti la giubba e la faccia infarina.

Put on the costume, and the face
in white powder.

La gente paga e rider vuole qua.

The people pay and laugh
when they please,

E se Arlecchin t'invola Colombina,

And if Harlequin invites Colombina away,

Ridi, Pagliaccio . . . e ognun applaudirà!

Laugh, Pagliaccio . . .
and everyone will applaud!

PAGLIACCI

Chapter Nine

Eclectic Buffet:
A Taste of Puccini

Aranci, datteri! caldi i marroni!

Oranges, dates, hot chestnuts!

Ninnoli, croci! Torroni!

Trinkets, crosses, nougat!

Panna montata!

Whipped cream!

Oh, la crostata!

Oh, fruit pies!

Caramelle!

Toffees!

Fiori alle belle!

Flowers for pretty girls!

Fringuelli, Passeri!

Finches, sparrows!

LA BOHÈME

WHAT SORT OF MENU CAN BEST REFLECT the varied works of Giacomo Puccini? One based on specialties of Lucca, the quaint, walled medieval city of Puccini's birth? A meal of Parisian dishes to honor *La Bohème*, the most-performed opera in the Met's distinguished repertoire? A sushi dinner to celebrate *Madama Butterfly*? How to choose a single theme for a man whose works are set in such far-flung times and places as ancient Peking, nineteenth-century Paris, early-twentieth-century Japan, and America's frontier.

In keeping with Puccini's sense of drama and theatrics, host an eclectic buffet inspired by the various exotic settings of his operas. Our Puccini party begins with a *Madama Butterfly* Sake Martini, a refreshing drink accented with ginger and cucumber and served with Asian-inspired appetizers like Black Lacquer Teriyaki Wings. The main course features Roman specialties like Scarpia's Saltimbocca, inspired by *Tosca's* locale. The meal ends with a not-to-be-believed delectable delight, *La Bohème* Fruit and Nut Fantasy.

Menu

COCKTAILS

Madama Butterfly *Sake Martini*

Chinese Iced Tea

APPETIZERS

Turandot *Tea Eggs*

Ping, Pang, and Pong Pork Nibbles

Black Lacquer Teriyaki Wings

BUFFET

Linguine Il Trittico *with Oranges, Apricots, and Almonds*

La Fanciulla del West *Seafood Chowder*

Scarpia's Saltimbocca

Spinach with Pine Nuts and Raisins

Roman-Style Crispy Artichokes

DESSERT

Monte Bianco

La Bohème *Fruit and Nut Fantasy*

PREVIOUS PAGES: *La Bohème*

Cocktails

YOU CAN MAKE THESE COCKTAILS TO ORDER OR, if you'd rather not spend the evening mixing drinks, make up a batch and put them in a pitcher for guests to help themselves.

MADAMA BUTTERFLY SAKE MARTINI
Serves 1

Sake, less forceful than vermouth, makes a marvelous martini. A hint of ginger adds just the right touch.

> 2 ounces vodka
>
> 1 tablespoon candied ginger, minced, plus more for garnish
>
> ½ ounce sake
>
> Cucumber slices, for garnish

Combine the vodka, ginger, sake, and crushed ice in a cocktail shaker and shake gently. Pour into a chilled martini glass and serve garnished with cucumber and candied ginger slices.

CHINESE ICED TEA
Serves 2

This drink is a *Turandot*-inspired variation on the classic Long Island Iced Tea cocktail. Use decorative lacquered chopsticks as stirrers, if you like.

> 2 jasmine tea bags, or 2 teaspoons loose tea
>
> 2 teaspoons sugar
>
> ½ ounce vodka
>
> ½ ounce gin
>
> ½ ounce rum
>
> ½ ounce Cointreau or other orange liqueur
>
> Orange slices, for garnish
>
> Lemon slices, for garnish

Steep the jasmine tea in ¾ cup boiling-hot water for 5 minutes. Remove the tea bags or strain, if using loose tea. Add the sugar and stir until dissolved. Allow to cool.

Place several ice cubes in two tall glasses. Divide the tea, vodka, gin, rum, and Cointreau between the glasses. Garnish with orange and lemon slices.

Birgit Nilsson in *Turandot*

Appetizers

TURANDOT TEA EGGS
Serves 6

The centuries-old Chinese technique of marinating eggs in tea and spices makes them look like beautiful marble. Different types of tea yield different colors. Green tea makes lovely yellow shades, Red Zinger purple hues, Lemon Zinger green striations, and black tea an assortment of golden-brown tones.

Accompany the tea eggs with tiny bowls of specialty salt, like orange-tinged Hawaiian salt or flavorful gray salt. Serve the eggs with flaked dulse, dried red seaweed that has a lovely purple cast and a delicate briny taste.

5 tea bags, or 5 heaping teaspoons loose tea

3 tablespoons soy sauce

2 tablespoons sugar

3 whole star anise, or 1 teaspoon anise seed

1 teaspoon black peppercorns

1 teaspoon whole cloves

1 teaspoon fennel seeds

One 2-inch stick of cinnamon

6 hard-boiled eggs

Salt, for serving

Steep the tea in 2 cups boiling-hot water in a bowl large enough to hold all the eggs. Remove the tea bags or strain, if using loose tea.

Stir in the soy sauce, sugar, star anise, peppercorns, cloves, fennel, and cinnamon. Set aside.

Gently tap the hard-boiled eggs on a hard surface until they are completely covered with fine crack lines. Place the eggs, still in their shells, in the tea mixture and marinate overnight in the refrigerator.

To serve, carefully peel the shell, leaving the inner membrane intact. Serve accompanied by salt.

"Do a little of what Shakespeare often does, when he brings in three or four extraneous types who drink, use bad language, and speak ill of the king."

GIACOMO PUCCINI
to librettists for *Turandot*

PING, PANG, AND PONG PORK NIBBLES
Serves 6

Always on hand with a snappy remark, the saucy characters Ping, Pang, and Pong are a delightful accent to *Turandot*, just as these nibbles are to the main meal.

Pork tenderloin bakes in about 20 minutes and easily slices into serving-sized portions, making it an absolutely perfect party food.

The plum peanut dipping sauce is a modern and lighter update of traditional Hoisin sauce.

> **1 pork tenderloin, about 1 pound**
> **Salt and freshly milled black pepper**
> **4 tablespoons honey**
> **1 tablespoon five-spice powder**
> **1 bunch scallions, finely sliced**
> **2 tablespoons toasted sesame oil**
> **3 cloves garlic, minced**
> **½ cup sherry**
> **¼ cup plum jelly**
> **¼ cup best-quality chicken stock**
> **¼ cup creamy peanut butter**
> **¼ cup soy sauce**
> **Red pepper flakes**

Preheat the oven to 425°F.

Liberally season the pork with salt and pepper. Drizzle 2 tablespoons of the honey over the pork and sprinkle on the five-spice powder. Put the pork onto a rack and cook for 18 to 22 minutes.

Meanwhile, in a medium saucepan over medium-high heat, sauté most of the scallions, reserving a portion for garnish, in sesame oil until golden, about 2 minutes. Add the garlic, sherry, plum jelly, chicken stock, peanut butter, soy sauce, and remaining 2 tablespoons of honey. Reduce heat to low and simmer for 10 minutes. Season to taste with red pepper flakes. Reserve.

Remove the pork from the oven and allow it to rest for 5 minutes before cutting. Arrange the pork slices on a serving platter, drizzled with the sauce and sprinkled with the reserved scallions.

BLACK LACQUER TERIYAKI WINGS
Serves 6 to 8

There is no getting around it; this *Madama Butterfly*–inspired nibble is a sticky mess. Slow-baked in sake-honey-teriyaki to sweet, gooey perfection and glistening—almost black—the wings smell as great as they look. Guests devour them. No guest of mine has ever complained about the mess.

You can serve them with a stack of warm wet tea towels like those you get in Japanese restaurants, but frankly, even my most proper pinkies-in-the-air guests end up just licking their fingers clean. These wings are that good.

This is a great party dish because the wings get even better after being left out on the buffet table for an hour or so.

> **24 chicken wings, about 4½ pounds, split at the joints**
> **5 to 7 large cloves garlic, minced**
> **1 cup teriyaki sauce**
> **¾ cup honey**
> **½ cup sake**
> **½ cup orange juice**
> **¼ cup finely minced candied or fresh ginger**
> **2 tablespoons sesame seeds**

Preheat the oven to 400°F. Line a roasting pan with aluminum foil and arrange the wings in a single layer on it.

Stir together the garlic, teriyaki sauce, honey, sake, orange juice, and ginger in a bowl until well combined.

Pour the mixture over the wings and bake for 1 hour. Raise the heat to 450°F, turn the wings over, and bake for an additional 30 minutes, until the wings are dark and the sauce is very thick.

Meanwhile, toast the sesame seeds in a dry skillet over medium heat until light golden, about 2 minutes.

To serve, transfer the wings to a serving platter and top with the sesame seeds.

NOTE: I often use candied or crystallized ginger as a substitute for fresh. Available in the spice section of most supermarkets, it lasts longer, has a more intense taste, and is less fibrous. It's much easier to chop, and I like the little bit of sweetness it adds.

Buffet

LINGUINE *IL TRITTICO* WITH ORANGES, APRICOTS, AND ALMONDS
Serves 6

A triptych of ingredients: Cointreau-spiked caramelized onions and sweet oranges are complemented by the slightly tart dried apricots to create a multilayered flavor.

- 1 pound linguine
- Salt
- 1/2 cup (1 stick) unsalted butter
- 1 large purple onion, thinly sliced
- 1/3 cup Cointreau or other orange liqueur
- 1 1/4 cups freshly squeezed orange juice
- 8 to 10 fresh or dried apricots, sliced
- 1 tablespoon light brown sugar
- 2 tablespoons minced best-quality candied orange peel, optional
- Freshly milled ground black pepper
- 1/2 teaspoon freshly grated nutmeg
- 1/2 cup freshly grated Parmesan cheese
- 1 cup almond slivers
- Zest of 1 orange, for garnish

Cook the linguine in plenty of salted water according to package directions.

Meanwhile, heat the butter in a large skillet over medium heat and sauté the onion until soft, about 5 minutes. Carefully add the Cointreau (it will splatter in the hot skillet) and simmer until reduced by half, about 2 minutes. Add 1/2 cup of the orange juice, the apricots, and brown sugar and stir until the sugar dissolves.

Slowly add the remaining 3/4 cup orange juice and simmer until the sauce turns golden, about 3 minutes. Remove from the heat, stir in the candied orange peel, if using, and generously season to taste with pepper.

Toss the sauce with the drained linguine and top with nutmeg, Parmesan, and almonds. Garnish with the zest.

> *"I consider myself happy to be able to say that I am among my friends, to whom I can speak in music with a certainty of being understood."*
>
> **GIACOMO PUCCINI,**
> referring to the Metropolitan Opera audience

LA FANCIULLA DEL WEST SEAFOOD CHOWDER
Serves 6

Fanciulla, an opera set in California's '49 gold rush, is celebrated with this Italian version of San Francisco seafood chowder. Ready in less than 30 minutes, this dish is chock-full of tender clams and mussels, succulent shrimp and sweet scallops. Guests gravitate to this hearty chowder, attracted by the aroma and vibrant mix of colors. The sourdough croutons add a delicious crunch, so be sure to make lots of them to absorb every drop of the mouthwatering broth.

> ½ cup extra-virgin olive oil
>
> 1 large Vidalia onion, diced
>
> 3 stalks celery with leaves, diced
>
> 4 cloves garlic, minced
>
> 1 cup dry white wine
>
> One 16-ounce can diced tomatoes
>
> 2 dozen littleneck clams, in shells, scrubbed
>
> 2 pounds mussels, in shells, scrubbed and debearded
>
> 8 ounces small shrimp, peeled and deveined
>
> 8 ounces sea scallops
>
> ¾ cup minced fresh parsley
>
> Salt and freshly milled black pepper
>
> 1 loaf sourdough bread

Heat ¼ cup of the olive oil in a large stockpot over medium heat and sauté the onions and celery until the onions are translucent, about 8 minutes. Add the garlic and sauté for another minute. Add the wine, raise the heat to high, and bring to a boil. Boil for 2 to 3 minutes to reduce the wine by about one-third.

Add the tomatoes, clams, and mussels and cook until the shells open, about 4 minutes. Add the shrimp and scallops and continue cooking until the scallops are opaque and cooked through, 1 to 2 minutes. Remove from heat, stir in ½ cup of the minced parsley, and season to taste with salt and pepper.

Cut the bread into bite-sized cubes. Drizzle with the remaining ¼ cup olive oil and toast under the broiler for 1 minute per side, or until golden.

Serve the chowder topped with the sourdough croutons and the remaining ¼ cup parsley.

SCARPIA'S SALTIMBOCCA
Serves 4 to 6

Saltimbocca got its name because it is so good it practically "jumps into the mouth." It's such a Roman favorite that it was probably on Puccini's mind when he wrote Scarpia's supper scene.

Saltimbocca is one of those classic recipes that should be in every home cook's repertoire. The thin slices of veal, sautéed in wine and accented with sage and prosciutto, pack lots of flavor even though there are relatively few ingredients.

> 3 very thin veal or chicken cutlets, about 6 ounces each
>
> Freshly milled black pepper
>
> Flour, for dredging
>
> 6 slices prosciutto
>
> 6 large fresh sage leaves, plus more for garnish
>
> 2 tablespoons unsalted butter
>
> ½ cup white wine

Season the cutlets with pepper and cut them in half lengthwise. Dredge each section in flour. Use a toothpick to secure 1 slice of prosciutto and 1 sage leaf to each cutlet section.

In a medium skillet melt the butter over medium-high heat until it begins to foam. Add the cutlets, prosciutto side down, and cook about 2 minutes. Turn and cook the other side for about 1 minute. Add the wine and simmer for 1 to 2 minutes.

Remove the toothpicks and place the cutlets on a serving platter topped with the sauce. Garnish with additional fresh sage leaves.

Hildegard Behrens and Plácido Domingo in *Tosca*

L'arte nel suo mistero

Art, in its mystery,

Le diverse bellezze insiem confonde:

Blends the different beauties together:

Ma nel ritrar costei

But in portraying this woman

Il mio solo pensiero, Tosca, sei tu!

My only thought is you, Tosca, it's you!

TOSCA

OPERA NOTE

Maria Callas sang only twenty-one times at the Metropolitan Opera in four roles: Norma, Lucia, Violetta in *La Traviata*, and Tosca. She played Tosca for her last appearance in 1965, opposite her acclaimed artistic partner, Tito Gobbi, as Scarpia.

There are many amusing Callas stories. Here's a foodie one. Callas was ill one evening, so her pal Marlene Dietrich, who prided herself on her gourmet cooking, brought her a cup of her laboriously made slow-simmered beef stock. Maria, unaware that it was homemade, tasted it and said, "Delicious! What brand of bouillon cubes do you use?"

"The Almighty touched me with His little finger and said: 'Write for the theatre—mind well, only for the theatre!'"

GIACOMO PUCCINI

SPINACH WITH PINE NUTS AND RAISINS
Serves 4

One bite and you'll be transported to Rome listening to the church bells near Castel Sant'Angelo. The raisins add sweetness and the pine nuts provide richness and crunch to the buttery spinach.

You'll make this classic Roman side dish again and again.

- ¼ cup pine nuts
- ¼ cup golden raisins
- 3 tablespoons unsalted butter
- 3 cloves garlic, thinly sliced
- 2½ pounds fresh spinach
- Salt and freshly milled black pepper

Place the pine nuts in a small nonstick skillet and toast them over medium heat for about 2 minutes until golden. Reserve. Soak the raisins in ¼ cup hot water while you cook the garlic.

Heat the butter in a large sauté pan over medium heat and sauté the garlic until soft, about 2 minutes. Drain the water from the raisins and pat dry with a paper towel.

Add the raisins and spinach to the pan, cover, and cook for about 2 minutes, until the spinach is tender. Remove from the heat and season to taste with salt and pepper.

Serve topped with the pine nuts.

ROMAN-STYLE CRISPY ARTICHOKES
Serves 6

In Italy this recipe is called *carciofi alla Giudea* or artichokes Jewish-style.

I like to imagine that artichokes prepared like these were among the foods in the basket Cavaradossi shares with Angelotti in the church of Sant'Andrea della Valle.

> 6 baby artichokes
>
> 2 lemons, quartered
>
> 1/2 cup extra-virgin olive oil
>
> Salt and freshly milled black pepper

Remove any tough outer leaves from the artichokes and cut off the thorny tops. Cut each artichoke in half and sprinkle with the juice of 1 or 2 of the lemon quarters to prevent darkening.

In a sauté pan over high heat, heat the oil until smoky, about 2 minutes. Place the artichokes in the pan and cook for about 4 minutes per side, or until they are tender and the edges have crisped. Transfer the artichokes to a paper-towel-lined plate to drain the excess oil.

To serve, arrange the artichokes on a serving platter, season to taste with salt and pepper, and garnish with the remaining lemon quarters.

Teresa Stratas and José Carreras in *La Bohème*

OPERA NOTE

In the film *Moonstruck*, Nicholas Cage's character, Ronny Cammareri, is an opera lover. In a recent chat with John Patrick Shanley, the Pulitzer Prize–winning playwright and Academy Award–winning screenwriter of the movie, I asked him why Ronny loved opera.

Shanley explained that, as a hot-tempered, highly dramatic Italian-American, Ronny would naturally have been an opera lover: "Opera resonated for Ronny. It was a symbol of the passion he craved in life."

Shanley chose *La Bohème*, an opera he had first seen in an amateur production, because he felt it "captures the romantic simplicity that is life and is filled with honest feelings."

Dessert

THESE TWO DESSERTS ARE INSPIRED BY THE LIST OF WARES the shopkeepers and street vendors hawk outside Café Momus in *La Bohème*—*"caldi i marroni . . . panna montata . . ."*

MONTE BIANCO
Serves 6

Monte Bianco, this classic Italian dessert made with creamy chestnuts and whipped cream, is a melt-in-your-mouth delight that looks like a snow-topped mountain. The "mountain" is made with a puree of roasted chestnuts and spices, and the "snow" is brandy-spiked whipped cream and sparkling meringue (think Act III in the Zeffirelli production!).

This festive, fun, impressive-looking dessert is easy to make, thanks to supermarket meringue cookies and ready-roasted chestnuts.

    2½ cups whole milk

    ¾ cup sugar

    2 tablespoons fennel seeds

    1 pound ready-roasted, peeled chestnuts

    2 ounces best-quality bittersweet chocolate,
        finely chopped

    ¼ cup plus 1 tablespoon brandy or rum

    1 teaspoon vanilla extract

    1 cup heavy cream

    3 to 4 vanilla meringue cookies, coarsely chopped

In a medium saucepan, combine the milk, ½ cup of the sugar, and fennel seeds in a medium saucepan and cook over low heat to release the fennel's flavor, about 5 minutes. Strain and return the liquid to the saucepan. Add the chestnuts and simmer for 20 minutes.

Put the warm chestnut mixture in a food processor with the chocolate, ¼ cup of the brandy, and the vanilla. Pulse to blend and then process until very smooth. Allow to cool to room temperature, then cover with plastic wrap and refrigerate for at least 1 hour and up to 2 days.

Just before serving, press the chestnut mixture through a potato ricer onto a serving platter, forming a mountain-shaped cone. Whip the cream with the remaining ¼ cup sugar in a large bowl with an electric mixer until peaks form. Stir in the remaining tablespoon of brandy. Top the chestnut "mountain" with the whipped cream and sprinkle with the meringue cookies.

Serve immediately.

OPERA NOTE

An amusing foodie scene occurs in Act I of *La Bohème* when Schaunard arrives bearing assorted comestibles. Schaunard tells his friends how he earned the money for the wine and food. He explains that he was hired by a wealthy Englishman to entertain the man's dying parrot. Asked to play for the bird until it died, the bored Schuanard cleverly hastened the bird's demise with poisoned parsley. His starving friends are too distracted setting the table and eating to pay any attention to his incredible tale.

LA BOHÈME FRUIT AND NUT FANTASY
Serves 12 to 14

You're going to love this wildly flavorful mix of oranges, dates, torrone, and bits of candy inspired by *La Bohème*. In one bite you get a little piece of hazelnut, sweet chocolate, pear, and dried fig, and then in the next bite a morsel of soft torrone, bittersweet chocolate, and dried cherries.

I'm eating some as I'm writing this, trying to capture the sweet, chewy, crunchy deliciousness on paper as I'm experiencing it. I'm not sure I can. It's just too good to describe. You'll have to make it yourself. You will be eternally grateful to me for introducing you to this refreshing, healthful, beautiful, unusual, festive dessert.

Although frequently served in private homes in Italy, it isn't usually available in restaurants there, so few Americans have ever tasted it.

    6 large dates, minced
    6 dried figs, minced
    ¼ pound candied orange peel, minced
    8 to 10 amaretti, minced
    1 cup minced assorted nuts such as hazelnuts, wal-
        nuts, and almonds
    ⅓ cup pine nuts
    8 ounces soft torrone, Italian nougat candy, minced
    2 ounces dark chocolate, finely chopped
    1 ounce milk chocolate, finely chopped
    10 dried apricots, minced
    ½ cup dried cherries or cranberries
    ¼ cup golden raisins
    2 fresh pears, peeled and diced
    2 fresh apples, peeled and diced
    1 cup orange juice
    ½ to 1 cup liqueur of your preference,
        such as limoncella or Amaretto

In a large bowl, combine the dates, figs, candied orange, and amaretti. Mix well to coat the fruit with the amaretti crumbs. This prevents the sticky dried fruit from clumping together.

Gently mix in the nuts and pine nuts. Add the torrone, chocolates, apricots, cherries, and raisins, and mix gently with your hands or a wooden spoon. Cover with plastic wrap and reserve in a cool dry place for up to 2 weeks.

Just before serving, combine the reserved mixture, the pears and apples, and the orange juice in a serving bowl. Splash on liqueur to taste.

La Bohème

Chapter Ten

Vodka Tasting with Russian Composers

Radostno, veselo v den sei
In joy and merriment
vmeste sbiraitesya drugi!
Gather round today, friends!

THE QUEEN OF SPADES

CELEBRATE THE WORKS OF RUSSIAN OPERA COMPOSERS, including Modest Petrovich Mussorgsky, Piotr Ilich Tchaikovsky, and Sergei Sergeievich Prokofiev, by hosting a vodka-tasting party. Vodka, the Russian national beverage, is also America's favorite mixed-drink ingredient, and you will thrill your guests with the delectable infusions you create mixing it with fresh fruit and zesty spices. Serve an assortment of Russia's favorite *zakuski* nibbles, such as easy-to-make Mushroom "Caviar" with Sweet Potato Blini and Three Oranges Tangy Vodka-Marinated Veggies. Before guests head home, offer them hot samovar tea sweetened with Russian jams to be sipped as they savor delicious Russian Sweet Bread with Orange Icing. *Priyatnogo Apetita!*

Menu

COCKTAILS

Fruit-Infused Vodka

Spice-Infused Vodka

Black Russian

White Russian

ZAKUSKI

Caviar with Buckwheat Blini

Smoked Salmon with Caper Cream

Three Oranges Tangy Vodka-Marinated Veggies

Golden Borscht Shots

Mushroom "Caviar" with Sweet Potato Blini

Seafood Smorgasbord with Garlic-Horseradish Potatoes

Radish Bites

Russian Sweet Bread with Orange Icing

PREVIOUS PAGES: *The Queen of Spades*

Cocktails

VODKA, DERIVED FROM THE RUSSIAN WORD *VODA*, FOR "WATER," was born there sometime between the ninth and twelfth centuries.

This clear, unaged distilled alcohol was originally made from potatoes, Russia's leading crop. Nowadays it is primarily made from grains like wheat, barley, and rye.

In the 1700s, the Russians discovered a method of purifying the flavor of the alcohol by using charcoal as a filter. They then further improved it by adding honey. Later experiments involved flavorings like dill, juniper, sage, and all sorts of fruits.

FRUIT-INFUSED VODKA

Plum, melon, and citrus are traditional Russian infusion favorites, but absolutely any fruit works. I know firsthand, because I've probably tried them all. Apples, apricots, bananas, blackberries, kiwis, mangoes, pomegranates, and raspberries—they are all wonderful.

You can infuse a whole bottle of vodka with one flavor or do what I do and divide the recipe to experiment with two or three different fruits or fruit combinations. Store the vodka-fruit mix in pint- or quart-sized canning-type mason jars or any sturdy glass container with a lid.

Nazdorovie!

> **One 750-ml bottle vodka**
> **4 cups fruit (any fruit or combination), chopped**
> **½ cup superfine sugar**
> **2 vanilla beans**

Combine ingredients in a glass container with a lid.

Refrigerate for at least 2 weeks. Strain and store the liquid in the freezer until ready to use.

Day mne pit!

Quickly, give me something to drink!

Day pit skoreye,

Quickly, a drink,

Il ya umru ot zazhdi

or I'll die of thirst,

Ot zhestokoy zhazhdi

a cruel thirst,

Ot smertelnowy zhazhdi

a deadly thirst!

LOVE FOR THREE ORANGES

War and Peace

ABSOLUTE ICE

Several vodka companies have sponsored "ice bars," drinking establishments where guests can sip icy-cold vodka in glasses made of ice, while standing in a room made entirely of ice. The walls are built of blocks of ice, the chairs are sculpted ice covered with fur throws, and of course the room's decorations are ice sculptures. Guests borrow snuggly capes and gloves to stay cozy.

One of the first and still trendiest is the Absolut Icebar in Jukkasjärvi, Sweden. Absolut's ice bar is filled with whimsical ice sculptures of Da Vinci's works. Their Quebec ice bar is housed in a hotel that is also made entirely of snow and ice. Stoli, too, opened an ice bar located in icy-cold Fairbanks, Alaska.

SPICE-INFUSED VODKA

You can flavor vodka with any spice or herb that strikes your fancy. Some traditional favorites are horseradish, chile pepper, and caraway seeds.

I especially like ginger, which I make with either ¼ cup diced ginger or 3 tablespoons of diced candied ginger. Mmm.

3 to 4 tablespoons spice (any spice or spice combination)

One 750-ml bottle vodka

Slightly crush the spice using a mortar and pestle, a meat tenderizer, or the back of a small skillet. Heat a small skillet over low heat and warm the spice for about 1 minute to release its full flavor.

Combine the vodka and spice in a glass container with a lid. Refrigerate for at least 2 weeks. Strain and store the liquid in the freezer until ready to use.

BLACK RUSSIAN
Serves 1

1¹/₂ ounces vodka

³/₄ ounce coffee liqueur such as Kahlúa

Grated bittersweet chocolate

Combine the vodka and liqueur with crushed ice in a shaker and mix well. Strain into a chilled short cocktail glass and top with a sprinkle of chocolate.

WHITE RUSSIAN
Serves 1

1¹/₂ ounces vodka

1 ounce white crème de cacao

³/₄ ounce heavy cream

Combine the vodka, crème de cacao, and heavy cream with crushed ice in a shaker and mix well. Strain into a chilled short cocktail glass.

Pej, Balaga, bej stakany!

Drink, Balaga. Smash the glasses.

Vot eta zhyzn'!

This is living!

WAR AND PEACE

OPERA NOTE

The Russians, in good spirits at having driven off the invading French, tease one another, especially Fyodor, who has been shot in the backside:

Tikhon: *I suppose our Fyodor Mikheich tended his wound with vodka.*

Chorus: *For external use, or did you drink it?*

Fyodor: *I mostly drank it.*

War and Peace

HOW TO MAKE A VODKA ICE BLOCK

For a showstopping presentation, serve a bottle of vodka frozen in a block of ice. You can decorate the ice by freezing amusing objects in it, such as music charms. Or echo the flavor, so when serving citrus-infused vodka, freeze lemon, lime, and orange slices into the ice block.

To make an ice block, place a bottle of vodka into an empty container large enough to hold it. Two-liter plastic soda or water bottles with their tops cut off are perfect for the average-sized bottle of vodka. Fill with water and freeze overnight or until solid.

When ready to serve, run hot water around the container until the ice block slips out or, if using a plastic disposable bottle, snip it off with shears. Set the ice-encased vodka bottle on an attractive cloth, over a platter, to collect the water as the ice melts.

You can even make an ice block around those adorable little airline-size bottles. Just put the bottle in an eight-ounce paper or plastic drinking cup, fill with water. Once the water has frozen, snip the cup off the ice block.

Zakuski

The United States government permits only sturgeon roe, or eggs, to be labeled simply as "caviar." All others must specify further by adding the name of the fish—salmon caviar comes from salmon, lumpfish caviar from, well, lumpfish, and so on.

The three main types of sturgeon caviar are beluga, considered the best, with large soft gray-black eggs; ossetra, with medium-sized gray to brown-gray eggs; and sevruga, with small gray eggs. There are many American-farmed sturgeon caviars on the market and conservation organizations encourage their use because sturgeon is endangered in the wild. Especially tasty is the caviar from California-farmed white sturgeon.

Sturgeon caviar may be the true Russian delicacy, but other types of caviar can be wonderful. My favorite is American salmon caviar, which has large red-orange eggs that pop with flavor when you bite into them.

CAVIAR WITH BUCKWHEAT BLINI
Serves 10 to 12, makes about 18 blini

Blini, or *blinchiki* in Russian, are tiny pancakes. Earthy and pleasingly grainy, buckwheat is the classic blini flour.

Consider preparing the blini in front of your guests. Unlike the cook in *Love for Three Oranges*, who shouts, "Impudent puppy! What are you doing here . . . I'll shake the life out of you! Creeping into my kitchen!" I enjoy guests in the kitchen.

It's a fun, informal start to the party. The guests feel special, more like family, when you invite them into your kitchen. There's an instant comradeship created with everyone eating warm blini just off the skillet and sipping shots of icy-cold vodka right from the freezer.

   1 cup whole milk

   4 eggs, separated

   1 cup buckwheat flour

   ⅓ cup honey

   2 teaspoons baking powder

   ½ teaspoon salt

   Zest of 1 lemon

   Vegetable or canola oil, for cooking the blini

   Crème fraîche, for serving

   3 ounces caviar, any type, for serving

   Lemon wedges, for serving

In a large bowl, using an electric mixer, blend the milk and egg yolks until well combined. Add the flour, honey, baking powder, salt, and zest and blend until well combined.

In a separate bowl, using an electric mixer, beat the egg whites until stiff peaks form. Fold the egg whites into the batter.

Preheat a scant amount of oil in a large nonstick skillet over medium-low heat. Place heaping tablespoons of batter onto the skillet to form 2½-inch blini. Cook until lightly browned, then turn and cook the other side.

You can serve the blini immediately or reserve them, covered, on a cookie sheet. Reheat them in a 300°F oven for a few minutes just before serving.

To serve, arrange the warm blini on a platter and top each with a dollop of crème fraîche and caviar. Provide lemon wedges on the side.

Felicity Palmer in *The Queeen of Spades*

SMOKED SALMON WITH CAPER CREAM
Serves 6 to 8

Silky salmon served with rich, tangy lemony caper crème fraîche—it's like a Baltic cruise for your taste buds!

Ask your bakery for *chornyi khleb*, the dark and richly delicious Russian black bread made with rye and molasses. As an ode to Tchaikovsky's *The Queen of Spades*, cut the bread into spade shapes with a specialty cookie-cutter.

> 1 teaspoon capers, drained
> ½ cup crème fraîche
> 1 teaspoon freshly squeezed lemon juice
> 12 thin slices black bread
> 3 ounces smoked salmon, sliced thinly
> Red onion, very finely sliced, for garnish
> Whole pink peppercorns, for garnish

In a small bowl, mash the capers with a fork. Add the crème fraîche and lemon juice and combine until well mixed.

Using a spade-shaped cookie-cutter or knife, cut the bread into serving-sized portions. Spread the bread with about 1 tablespoon of the crème fraîche mixture and top with a slice of salmon. Garnish with red onions and pink peppercorns.

Raw, Smoked, or Cured

There are many types of raw and smoked salmon. Gravlax is a Swedish method of curing raw salmon in sugar, salt, and dill brine. Lox is a brine-cured cold-smoked salmon.

Nova Scotia salmon is also cold-smoked, but is usually less salty than lox. The name comes from the days when most salmon in the States came from the Nova Scotia area.

Fresh salmon can be raw-cured or smoked. There are two ways to smoke. Hot smoking uses higher heat for less time, usually only six to twelve hours. Cold smoking, at low heat, can take from one day to three weeks.

> *"Do you know it must really be good, because in certain places I can't play because I feel I am going to cry."*
>
> **PIOTR TCHAIKOVSKY,**
> on *The Queen of Spades*

THREE ORANGES TANGY VODKA-MARINATED VEGGIES

Serve 8 to 10

Pickles are delicious, crunchy, and tangy, but most of us are stuck on only cucumber pickles. Here is the perfect vodka-spiked marinade to widen your pickle horizons. In less than thirty minutes you'll enjoy a mix of orange-flavored spicy sweet pickled veggies. Try using one of the many flavored vodkas in this recipe; I especially like using citrus or pepper vodka.

2 large carrots, trimmed

Freshly squeezed juice of 3 oranges, about ¾ cup

½ cup vodka, plain or flavored

¼ cup white wine vinegar

3 tablespoons sugar

1 tablespoon kosher or coarse sea salt

1 tablespoon whole cloves

1 tablespoon whole allspice

½ teaspoon red pepper flakes

1 bay leaf

½ pound fresh pearl onions, peeled and trimmed

½ pound string beans

Zest of 1 lemon, for garnish

Using a vegetable peeler, make long, wide carrot slices. Soak the slices in ice water while you prepare the other ingredients.

Combine the orange juice, vodka, vinegar, sugar, salt, cloves, allspice, red pepper flakes, bay leaf, and onions in a large saucepan. Simmer the onions over medium heat until just tender, about 10 minutes. Using a slotted spoon, remove the onions and put them on a serving platter.

Add the string beans to the hot liquid. Simmer until just tender, about 2 minutes. Remove with a slotted spoon and add them to the serving platter.

Simmer the carrot slices in the hot liquid until tender, less than 1 minute. Remove with a slotted spoon and add to the serving platter.

Garnish the vegetables with lemon zest and serve.

Vlyubis v tri apelsina!

You will fall in love with three oranges!

Vlyubis v tri apelsina!

You will fall in love with three oranges!

Vlyubis v tri apelsina!

You will fall in love with three oranges!

LOVE FOR THREE ORANGES

HANDS ON

Buy a box of inexpensive thin surgical gloves from the pharmacy. They are great for cutting foods like beets, which can stain your fingers, or garlic, which leaves odors. They'll also protect you from the hot oil in chile peppers, which can burn your eyes if you accidentally touch them after handling hot chiles.

War and Peace

GOLDEN BORSCHT SHOTS
Serves 10 to 12

A lighter, more sophisticated version of the Russian classic, this golden beet soup is delectable. Use a flavored vodka like pepper or vanilla to add your own signature to the recipe. Serve the soup warm in small espresso cups or shot glasses and pair it with an icy-cold shot of vodka.

> 2 tablespoons extra-virgin olive oil
>
> 1 large Vidalia onion, chopped
>
> 3 large leeks, chopped
>
> 4 to 6 golden beets, about 2 pounds, sliced
>
> ¼ cup vodka, plain or flavored
>
> 3 cups best-quality vegetable or chicken stock
>
> Salt and freshly milled black pepper
>
> 1 cup finely chopped beet greens or Swiss chard
>
> Sour cream, for serving
>
> Fresh chives, finely minced, for serving

Heat the oil in a stockpot over medium heat and sauté the onion in the oil until golden, 6 to 8 minutes. Add the leeks and beets and continue cooking for about 5 minutes.

Stir in the vodka and simmer until reduced by half. Add the stock and salt and pepper to taste, and cook until the beets are tender, about 10 minutes. Remove the pot from heat and gently stir in the beet greens. Allow to cool slightly and coarsely puree in a food processor.

Serve topped with a dollop of sour cream and sprinkle of chives.

MUSHROOM "CAVIAR" WITH SWEET POTATO BLINI
Serves 12

Poor-man's "caviar," called *gribnaya ikra* in Russian, is a mix of mushrooms accented with the bite of garlic and the liveliness of citrus in a creamy dill sauce. This mushroom lover's nibble tastes even better the next day. If you want to skip the blini, you can serve the "caviar" with veggie chips or just eat it plain by the spoonful. Don't miss this one.

FOR THE "CAVIAR"

3 tablespoons unsalted butter

3 large scallions, white and green parts, finely sliced

1/2 onion, minced

3/4 pound assorted mushrooms, finely chopped

1/2 teaspoon salt, plus more if needed

1/2 cup sour cream

3 tablespoons minced fresh dill, or 1 tablespoon dried, plus more for garnish

3 to 4 cloves garlic, finely minced

Freshly squeezed juice of 1 lemon

Freshly milled black pepper

FOR THE BLINI

2 medium sweet potatoes

1 cup whole milk

2 large eggs

2 tablespoons sugar

3 tablespoons unsalted butter, softened

1 1/2 cups all-purpose flour

1 tablespoon baking powder

1 teaspoon salt

1/4 cup vegetable oil

For the "caviar," melt the butter in a medium-sized skillet over medium heat and sauté the scallions and onion. Add the mushrooms and salt and cook, stirring occasionally, until the mushrooms are tender, about 5 minutes. Remove from heat and remove any excess liquid with a teaspoon.

In a serving bowl combine the sour cream, dill, garlic, and lemon juice. Add the warm mushroom mixture and season to taste with salt and pepper. Reserve while you make the blini.

For the blini, boil the potatoes until tender. Peel them while they are still warm. Puree the potatoes in a food processor with the milk, eggs, sugar, and butter until well combined. Slowly add the flour, baking powder, and salt.

Heat the oil in a nonstick skillet over medium-low heat. Drop tablespoon-sized amounts of the batter onto the skillet and spread each with the back of a spoon to form roughly 2 1/2-inch blini. Cook until golden, turn, and cook on the other side.

You may serve the blini immediately or reserve them, covered, on a cookie sheet and reheat them in a 300°F oven for a few minutes.

Arrange the warm blini, topped with a dollop of the mushroom "caviar" and a sprinkle of dill, on a serving platter.

OPERA NOTE

"The summer here is really wonderful. The flowers are abundant. Plenty of everything. Yesterday, half an hour before dinner when I went for a stroll, I found several lovely white mushrooms."

—Piotr Tchaikovsky

Tchaikovsky, like so many Russians of his time, enjoyed gathering wild mushrooms and often wrote about them to his brother Modest. While working in Frolovskoie on *The Queen of Spades*, he took daily recreational walks searching them out.

SEAFOOD SMORGASBORD WITH GARLIC-HORSERADISH POTATOES
Serves 8 to 10

A gorgeous platter of smoked fish and marinated herring is complemented by a tangy horseradish-spiked potato medley—perfect nibbles to enjoy with vodka.

  2 tablespoons olive oil

  1½ pounds small potatoes, such as red, purple, or fingerling, cut in half

  8 to 10 cloves garlic, unpeeled

  ½ teaspoon kosher salt

  ½ cup sour cream or crème fraîche

  2 tablespoons finely minced fresh chives, or 1 teaspoon dried

  1 tablespoon grated fresh horseradish, or 1 teaspoon prepared

  Salt and freshly milled black pepper

  1 whole smoked trout

  1 pound assorted smoked fish such as sea bass, sable, sturgeon, and mackerel

  ¼ pound vinegar-marinated herring

  1 cucumber, peeled and sliced

  1 pint grape tomatoes

  Black and rye breads

  Butter

  2 tablespoons finely minced fresh dill, or 1 teaspoon dried

Preheat the oven to 375°F.

Coat a small nonstick baking pan with 1 tablespoon of the oil. Arrange the potatoes, cut side down, on the pan. Scatter the garlic cloves around the potatoes. Drizzle with the remaining tablespoon of oil and sprinkle with kosher salt.

Bake for about 30 minutes, until the potatoes are tender. Allow to cool slightly.

Remove the garlic cloves, peel, and mash the flesh in a small bowl. Add the sour cream and chives. Season with the horseradish and salt and pepper to taste.

To serve, arrange the fish, cucumber, tomatoes, breads, butter, and potatoes on a large serving platter or cutting board. Top each potato half with the sour cream mixture and sprinkle with the dill.

RADISH BITES
Serves 6

This is an uptown Manhattan version of a classic radish salad very popular in the Russian section of Brighton Beach, Brooklyn. The creamy, sweet topping mellows the usual bite of raw radishes. Enjoy them with an icy-cold shot of pepper or ginger vodka.

  2 tablespoons sour cream

  1 scallion, finely minced

  Pinch of sugar

  Salt and freshly milled black pepper

  6 red radishes, cut in half

  2 tablespoons finely minced fresh dill, for garnish

In a small bowl, combine the sour cream, scallion, sugar, and salt and pepper to taste.

Arrange the radish halves on a serving platter and top with a dollop of the sour cream mixture. Garnish with dill.

Ne tuzhy, druzhok!

Don't grieve, my friend!

Vot pakushajte, barin:

kartoshki razhnejush'ije!

Get some of these down you, Sir: tasty potatoes!

Ty pakushaj! Vot tak-ta.

Take one! That's the way.

WAR AND PEACE

RUSSIAN SWEET BREAD WITH ORANGE ICING
Makes 24 mini muffin-sized breads

Kulich, fruit and spice bread, is a Russian Easter tradition. It's baked in a tall cylindrical pan and comes out looking like a chef's hat. Then it's glazed and topped with red roses.

Here's a modern update of the delectable treat using a mini muffin pan. Each sweet bread comes out looking like a tiny version of the tall classic. For a nod to tradition, serve them on a platter decorated with a single red rose.

- 1/4 cup finely diced assorted dried fruit such as apricots, apples, golden raisins, and cranberries
- 1/4 cup rum or sweet sherry
- 1/2 cup whole milk, warm
- 1/3 cup granulated sugar
- 2 packets active dry yeast, about 1/2 ounce total
- 2 1/2 cups all-purpose flour, plus more if needed
- 5 tablespoons unsalted butter, melted
- 1 large egg
- 2 large egg yolks
- 1 tablespoon ground cardamom
- 1 tablespoon vanilla extract
- 1/2 tablespoon ground mace
- 1/2 teaspoon salt
- 3 tablespoons finely minced candied orange peel, or the zest of 1 orange
- 1/2 cup almond slivers, plus more for garnish
- 1/2 cup confectioners' sugar
- 2 teaspoons orange juice or milk

Preheat the oven to 350°F and place a rack in the center position.

Mix the dried fruit and rum in a small bowl. Reserve.

Stir the milk, granulated sugar, and yeast together in a large bowl. Add 1 cup of the flour, the butter, egg, egg yolks, cardamom, vanilla, mace, and salt and, using an electric mixer, blend until well combined.

Gradually add the remaining 1 1/2 cups flour, beating well after each addition. Add the candied orange peel and almonds and continue mixing, adding a bit more flour, if needed, until the dough is smooth and satiny.

Divide the dough into 24 golf-ball-sized portions. Generously grease a mini muffin pan and place the dough balls in it. Bake for about 20 minutes, or until golden. Allow to cool.

Whisk the confectioners' sugar with the orange juice in a small bowl until smooth. Glaze each sweet bread with the sugar mixture and top with a few almond slivers.

> "The time is past when music was written for a handful of aesthetes. Today vast crowds of people have come face to face with serious music and are waiting with eager impatience. . . . The masses want great music, great events, great love, lively dances. They understand far more than some composers think, and want to deepen their understanding."
>
> **SERGEI PROKOFIEV**

Samovars

SAMOVARS HAVE BEEN ASSOCIATED WITH CONVERSATION AND FRIENDSHIP since their invention in the late 1700s. Russians sip cup after cup of tea from samovars while enjoying long, leisurely chats.

A samovar is a combination hot water dispenser and tea maker. The top portion is a teapot, which brews very concentrated tea. The gorgeous urn-shaped bottom section heats the water. Guests pour some concentrate into their cups and then dilute it to taste with hot water.

Samovars, the traditional Russian wedding gift of the nineteenth century, were made of copper and charcoal heated. These lovely antiques make handsome dining room decorations.

Invest in a modern samovar. There are many fine electric stainless steel models to choose from. It's a sophisticated way to serve tea, especially for large gatherings.

Prash'aj, rib'ata.

Farewell, my friends.

Za zdarovje! Ura!

Here's to your health!

WAR AND PEACE

AHH SWEET TEA

In *War and Peace*, even as Akhrosimova and Pierre Bezukhov discuss Natasha's infidelity, her father's failing estate, and Anatoly's bigamy, they pause for tea: "You're welcome to stay for tea, if you like."

Russians often sweeten their tea with jam, not sugar. Favorite jam flavors to pair with tea are cherry and raspberry, but almost any flavor livens up black tea and adds an authentic finale to your vodka-tasting party.

> *"Opera and only opera brings you close to people, allies you with a real public, makes you the property not merely of separate little circles but—with luck—of the whole nation."*
>
> **PIOTR TCHAIKOVSKY**

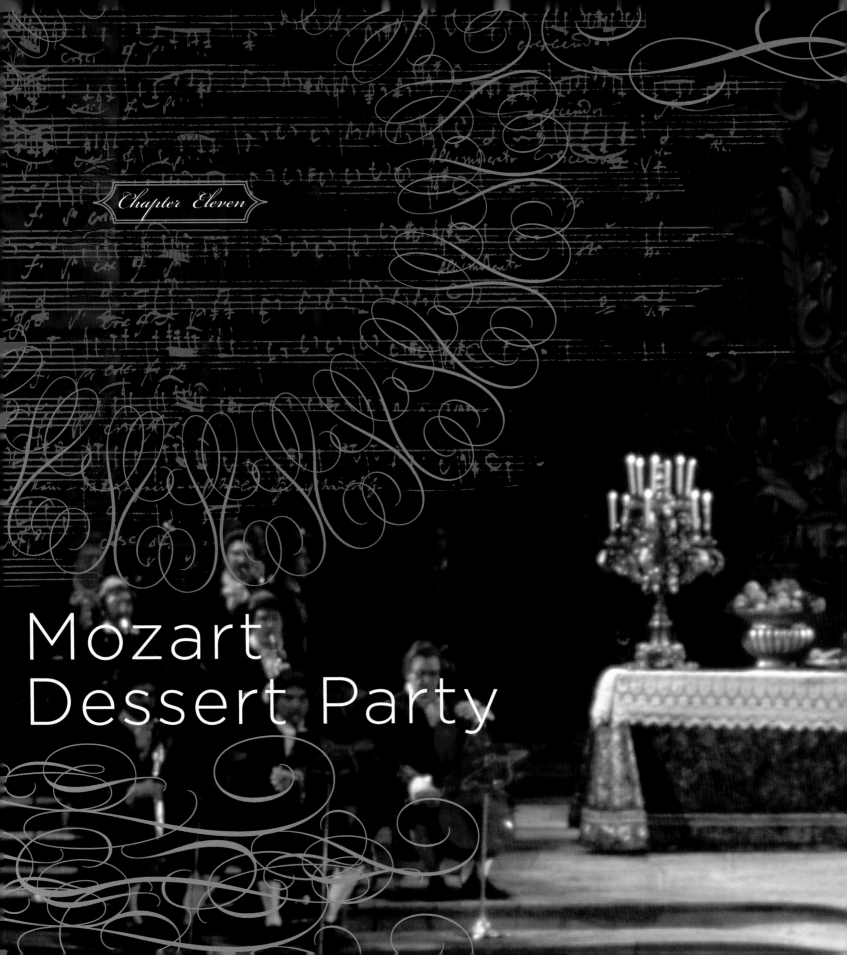

Chapter Eleven

Mozart
Dessert Party

Senza alcun ordine

Let the dancing

La danza sia;

Be spontaneous.

Chi'l minuetto,

They can do the minuet,

Chi la follia,

The caper,

Chi l'alemana

Or the waltz,

Farai ballar.

Just as you like.

DON GIOVANNI

MOZART'S BIRTHPLACE, AUSTRIA, IS RENOWNED FOR ITS DESSERTS, so it is only fitting to honor the maestro with a dessert party. It is a festive and unusual way to entertain. Maybe it's the sugar high, but I find that guests are always particularly gregarious and cheery at these gatherings. The combination of flavorful sweets and dessert wines will create a sure-to-please event that your friends will be talking about for weeks to come.

This chapter includes modern updates on classic Viennese specialties such as Sachertorte and linzertorte, as well as sweets inspired by Mozart's operas. You'll love the delectable *Così Fan Tutte* Chocolate Passion Fruit Fondue, the flavorful Harem Honey Custard, and the *Idomeneo* Dates with Wine and Spices, a dessert based on an authentic ancient Roman recipe. The *Don Giovanni* aria *"Fin ch'han dal vino"* inspires a simple yet elegant Pomegranate Wine Ice, and *Le Nozze di Figaro*, which is set in Spain, fosters Figaro's Orange Cake. For an intermezzo from sweets, you'll enjoy the wildly delicious *Magic Flute* Savory Surprise, a long sandwich-style loaf decorated to look like a flute. Add a festive musical touch to your dessert buffet table by decorating with any music-themed items you may own such as music boxes, snow globes, holiday ornaments, or vintage sheet music and opera programs.

Menu

BUFFET

Miniature Sachertorte

Linzertorte Music Bars

Così Fan Tutte *Chocolate Passion Fruit Fondue*

Idomeneo *Dates with Wine and Spices*

Pomegranate Wine Ice

Figaro's Orange Cake

Harem Honey Custard

Magic Flute *Savory Surprise*

PREVIOUS PAGES: **Don Giovanni**

Buffet

DESSERT WINE, OR "LATE-HARVEST WINE," AS IT IS ALSO CALLED, is made from grapes picked at the end of the growing season. The best dessert wines are made from grapes infected with a fungus that's poetically termed "noble rot" (*Botrytis cinerea*). This causes the grapes to shrivel while they're still on the vine, concentrating their flavor and sweetness.

Ice wine, or *Eiswein* in German, is made with grapes left on the vine even longer than late-harvest wines—until after the first frost. These wines are even more labor-intensive than late-harvest wines because the grapes must be hand-picked when the air temperature is between 8 and 14°F, which means workers must often gather them at night. Then the grapes must be quickly pressed while still frozen, a process that concentrates the acids, sugars, and flavor.

Ice wines are bursting with the flavor of honeyed fruit, citrus flowers, and aromatic spices. Their natural acidity balances their sweetness so they are always refreshing to the palate.

Don't be shocked by the high price of ice wines. It is due largely to the labor required to pick and press the fragile cold grapes. Fine ice wine is a gourmet delight well worth the price.

MINIATURE SACHERTORTE
Serves 12

Sachertorte, one of Austria's most famous desserts, was created in the 1830s by baker Franz Sacher.

Here I've updated the classic recipe by baking it as individual muffin-sized portions. The moist, light cake is topped with a glistening chocolate icing and served with a dollop of warm Cointreau-spiked apricot jam.

> 10 tablespoons unsalted butter, at room temperature, plus more for the pan
>
> ¾ cup superfine sugar
>
> 11 ounces bittersweet chocolate
>
> 1 cup all-purpose flour
>
> 8 eggs, separated
>
> ½ cup granulated sugar
>
> ¾ cup best-quality apricot jam
>
> ¼ cup Cointreau or other orange liqueur
>
> Whipped cream, for serving

Preheat the oven to 350°F and place the rack in the center position. Generously butter a 12-muffin pan.

In a large bowl using an electric mixer, beat the butter and superfine sugar until creamy, about 2 minutes. Melt 7 ounces of the chocolate and add it to the butter mixture, then add the flour and mix until well blended. Add the yolks of 6 of the eggs, one at a time, beating well after each addition. Discard the extra 2 yolks or reserve them for another use.

In a separate bowl using an electric mixer, beat the 8 egg whites until stiff peaks form. Add the egg whites to the chocolate batter, a little at a time, until just incorporated.

Divide the mixture into the prepared muffin pan and bake until a toothpick stuck into the center comes out clean, about 25 minutes. Allow to cool before serving.

Meanwhile, for the icing, in a medium saucepan over medium heat, melt the granulated sugar in ⅓ cup water. Melt the remaining chocolate and add it to the sugar syrup, and bring the icing to a low boil. Stir with a wooden spoon for about 2 minutes, or until the icing is glossy. Add a few drops of boiling water if the icing becomes too thick or to dissolve any sugar crystals that might form.

In a small saucepan over medium heat, heat the apricot jam and Cointreau until warm.

To serve, spoon the apricot sauce onto each serving plate and top with a muffin. Ice the muffins with the chocolate icing and top with a dollop of whipped cream.

LINZERTORTE MUSIC BARS
Makes 18 bars

Linzertorte, created in the late 1600s in Linz, Austria, is impressive yet easy to make. The rich, nutty dough comes together quickly in the food processor, and the jam filling is store-bought. Instead of the traditional tart pan, I use a rectangular baking pan and then cut the linzertorte into small individual-sized squares, which are better suited to a buffet. Instead of the usual lattice top crust, try small cookie-cutter shapes as a topping. Cookie-cutters come in music notes or instrument shapes, an amusing choice that hits the perfect note for a Mozart dessert party.

¾ cup almonds

¾ cup hazelnuts

¼ cup granulated sugar, plus more for sprinkling

1 teaspoon vanilla extract

1 teaspoon salt

½ teaspoon ground cinnamon

¼ teaspoon ground allspice

¼ teaspoon ground cloves

Zest of 1 lemon

¾ cup all-purpose flour

3 large eggs

¾ cup (1½ sticks) unsalted butter, cut into chunks, plus more for the pan

1 cup raspberry or red currant jam or preserves

Confectioners' sugar, optional

In a food processor, combine the almonds and hazelnuts and process just until finely ground. Heat the ground nuts in a dry skillet over medium heat, stirring, until lightly toasted, about 2 minutes. Allow to cool, and return them to the processor. Add the granulated sugar, vanilla, salt, cinnamon, allspice, cloves, and zest and pulse until well combined.

Slowly add the flour, pulsing until incorporated. Add 2 of the eggs and the butter, pulsing until well combined. The dough will be crumbly. Beat the remaining egg in a bowl and reserve.

Refrigerate the dough, covered with plastic, for at least 4 hours, or place it in the freezer for 1 hour, until very firm.

Preheat the oven to 350°F. Lightly butter a 10-inch-square baking pan.

Press ¾ of the dough into the prepared pan. Spread evenly with the jam, extending the jam to the edges of the pan.

Roll the remaining dough into a ⅛-inch-thick disc on a lightly floured surface and, using an assortment of small cookie-cutters, cut out as many topping shapes as possible. Reroll the scraps and cut out more symbols.

Arrange the topping shapes in about eighteen 2-inch serving-sized clusters over the jam and carefully brush them with egg. Sprinkle the shapes with granulated sugar and bake for about 35 minutes, or until light golden. Set the pan on a rack to cool, then cut the linzertorte into about 18 sections. Top with confectioners' sugar, if using.

Tocca e bevi!

Toast and drink!

Bevi e tocca

Drink and toast!

COSÌ FAN TUTTE

È mezz'ora che sbatto;

I've been beating this for half an hour,

Il cioccolatte è fatto, ed a me tocca

And now the chocolate's ready;
yet though my tongue's

Restar ad odorarlo a secca bocca?

Hanging out, must I just stand
and smell it?

Non è forse la mia come la vostra,

Aren't my tastes just like yours?

O garbate signore,

O dearest ladies, you have the substance

Che a voi dessi l'essenza, e a me l'odore?

And I only the smell!

Per Bacco, vo' assaggiarlo.

Damn it, I'm going to try it.

Com'è buono!

Delicious!

COSÌ FAN TUTTE

COSÌ FAN TUTTE CHOCOLATE PASSION FRUIT FONDUE
Serves 6

This fondue is inspired by the scene in Act I of *Così Fan Tutte* when Despina, the maid, simply can't resist a taste of the hot chocolate she's preparing for her mistress.

Passion fruit liqueur adds just the right spirit to the bitter-sweet chocolate sauce. It's an irresistible partner for sweet ripe pineapple.

For a decorative touch, garnish the table with miniature pineapples or the spiky pineapple tops.

> ¼ cup heavy cream
>
> 8 ounces bittersweet or semisweet chocolate, finely chopped
>
> 3 tablespoons unsalted butter
>
> ¼ cup passion fruit liqueur such as Alizé
>
> 1 ripe pineapple, peeled, cored, and cut into bite-sized sections
>
> 2 tablespoons brown sugar, optional

Warm the cream in a small saucepan or fondue pot over low heat. While still on low heat add the chocolate and butter and stir until creamy. Remove from the heat and stir in the liqueur.

Serve the pineapple sections, sprinkled with brown sugar, if using, accompanied by the chocolate sauce for dipping. If you like, present the skewers by inserting them into a section of the pineapple skin and decorate the serving platter with the pineapple top or with miniature pineapples.

IDOMENEO DATES WITH WINE AND SPICES
Serves 6

The ancient Greeks believed that dates were powerful aphrodisiacs. I'm not certain of that claim, but I am sure you'll be passionate about this recipe. Dates have a nice dense, chewy quality with a rich, almost smoky flavor, accented here in port flavored with aromatic spices. The silky, sweet dates are served with creamy mascarpone and topped with just a touch of fragrant orange zest.

> 12 Medjool dates
>
> 1 cup port wine
>
> 2 tablespoons honey
>
> ¹/₂ teaspoon pink peppercorns
>
> 1 bay leaf
>
> Zest of 1 orange, for serving
>
> Mascarpone cheese, for serving

With a sharp knife, make a small cut lengthwise through the top of each date and remove the pit.

Simmer the port, honey, peppercorns, and bay leaf in a small saucepan over low heat for about 15 minutes, until thickened. Place the dates in the pan and simmer until warm, about 5 minutes. Remove the dates with a slotted spoon and allow them to cool enough to handle. You may peel the skin, if you like, but it is not necessary.

Arrange the dates on a serving platter and drizzle any remaining wine sauce over the tops. Sprinkle with the orange zest. Serve with mascarpone.

Idomeneo

HOT HOT HOT

Back in the late eighteenth century, when *Così* was written, chocolate was served only as a hot beverage. The arts of making candy and baking with chocolate hadn't yet been discovered.

Hot chocolate and hot cocoa are not the same. Hot cocoa is made with cocoa powder, while hot chocolate is made by whisking bittersweet chocolate into warm milk.

Serve guests a pot of authentic hot chocolate for your Mozart dessert party. You can add a dash of vanilla, cinnamon, cloves, or even a pinch of cayenne. A splash of liqueur like Tia Maria is also nice. In Spain hot chocolate is served thickened with cornstarch or rice flour. No matter what you add, the two secrets to unforgettable European-style hot chocolate are, first, use the best-quality bittersweet chocolate with at least 80 percent cocoa and, second, be sure to whisk briskly.

Serve the hot chocolate unsweetened, accompanied by decorative sugar cubes. Set out an assortment of your vintage chocolate pots and antique sugar bowls if you're a collector.

Finch'han dal vino

Now prepare

Calda la testa,

A great feast

Una gran festa

Until the wine

Fà preparer.

Makes all heads reel.

Se trovi in piazza

If on the way

Qualche ragazza,

You meet some young lady,

Teco ancor quella

Try also to bring

Cerca menar.

Her along.

DON GIOVANNI

POMEGRANATE WINE ICE
Serves 10 to 12

You'd never imagine three ingredients and only a few minutes' assembly could result in such amazing flavor. This elegant dessert, with a refreshing, light hint of wine and the tart-sweet tang of pomegranate, is like a grown-up's gourmet slushy.

1¼ cups sugar
16 ounces pomegranate juice
2 cups white wine
Pomegranate seeds, for garnish

In a medium saucepan over high heat, bring the sugar and ¼ cup water to a boil. Reduce the heat to medium, add the juice, and let simmer for about 10 minutes. Remove from the heat and stir in the wine. Allow to cool to room temperature.

Pour the mixture into a shallow metal pan and freeze for at least 12 hours. Before serving, mash the mixture with a fork until it resembles a slushy.

To serve, spoon the ice into martini glasses or champagne flutes and top with pomegranate seeds.

FIGARO'S ORANGE CAKE
Serves 10

This cake is super moist and simple to make. The brilliant tart-sweet Seville oranges yield astonishing flavor in both the batter and glaze. As popular in Spain in Figaro's day as it is today, this delicious cake would have surely been served at his wedding feast.

You're probably already familiar with Seville oranges. They are the primary ingredient in orange marmalade, in orange-flower water, and in the liqueurs Cointreau, Grand Marnier, and Curaçao.

You can substitute navel oranges and still have a scrumptious cake.

½ cup (1 stick) unsalted butter, softened

1 cup plus 2 tablespoons granulated sugar

4 eggs, separated

Zest and juice of 3 Seville or navel oranges

2 cups all-purpose flour

2 tablespoons baking powder

½ teaspoon salt

¼ cup whole milk, at room temperature

2 cups confectioners' sugar, plus more as needed

Almond slices

Preheat the oven to 375°F. Butter and flour a 9-inch cake pan and set aside.

In a large bowl, using an electric mixer, beat the butter and 1 cup of the granulated sugar together on high speed until light and fluffy, about 5 minutes. Add the egg yolks, one at a time, mixing well after each addition. Add two-thirds of the orange zest and then two-thirds of the juice.

Slowly stir in the flour, baking powder, salt, and milk. Mix on low speed until combined.

In another bowl, whip the egg whites using an electric mixer set on high. When the egg whites begin to get frothy, sprinkle with the remaining 2 tablespoons granulated sugar. Continue beating until the egg whites hold a stiff peak.

Gently stir about ¼ of the whites into the batter to lighten it. Fold in the remaining whites until just combined, being careful not to overmix. Pour the batter into the prepared pan and bake for about 30 minutes, or until golden and a toothpick inserted in the center comes out clean.

Cool the cake on a rack in the pan for 10 minutes, then invert and cool completely.

To make the glaze, whisk together the confectioners' sugar and the remaining orange juice until smooth, adding more confectioners' sugar if the glaze is too thin. Pour half of the glaze over the top of the cooled cake, allowing it to drip down the sides. Let the cake stand for 10 minutes, then top with the remaining glaze. Garnish with the remaining orange zest and almond slices.

Ma, signore,

My lord,

Se in lui parla il vino!

It's the wine in him talking!

LE NOZZE DI FIGARO

HAREM HONEY CUSTARD
Serves 6

I'm hopelessly clumsy, so one should never trust me anywhere near one of those crème brûlée torches. I had to figure out my own way to get that dark-colored topping on custard and have hit on a perfect method. In this recipe, the toasted almonds float up to the top of the custard during baking, giving it a dazzling, wonderfully golden crust.

Good looks are not all this dessert has going for it. Based on Turkish milk pudding recipes, this creamy, nutty, but not-too-rich dessert has a pleasing bite of peppercorns and an outstanding smooth texture. It will become one of your standby sweets, as it's quickly made with items you almost always have on hand.

½ cup finely ground almonds

2 cups whole milk

½ teaspoon freshly grated nutmeg

½ teaspoon ground allspice

Freshly milled five-color peppercorns

¼ cup plus 2 tablespoons honey

Pinch of salt

Unsalted butter, for the ramekins

3 eggs

1 egg white

3 tablespoons nut liqueur such as Amaretto

In a dry nonstick skillet, toast the ground almonds over medium heat for 2 to 3 minutes until golden. Reserve 2 tablespoons of nuts for garnish.

Place the remaining almonds and the milk, nutmeg, allspice, and pepper to taste in a saucepan over medium-low heat. Gently simmer the mixture for about 10 minutes to reduce the milk and infuse the flavors. Remove from heat and stir in ¼ cup of the honey and the salt. Allow to cool to room temperature.

Preheat the oven to 325°F and place the rack in the center position. Lightly grease six ½-cup ramekins and place them in a deep baking pan.

In a small bowl, beat the eggs and egg white and whisk them into the milk custard until well incorporated. Pour the custard into the ramekins. Fill the baking pan with hot water until it reaches halfway up the sides of the ramekins. Cover the pan with aluminum foil.

Bake the custards for about 40 minutes. Turn off the heat, but leave the ramekins in the oven for another 10 to 15 minutes, until set and firm.

While the custard is cooling in the oven, make the sauce. Mix the remaining 2 tablespoons honey with the liqueur in a small bowl.

To serve, leave the custards in the ramekins or, if you prefer, invert them onto a plate, then invert again onto serving plates so that they rest golden side up. Drizzle with the honey-liqueur sauce and top with the reserved almonds.

"I pay no attention whatever to anybody's praise or blame. I simply follow my own feelings."

WOLFGANG AMADEUS MOZART

MAGIC FLUTE SAVORY SURPRISE
Serves 10 to 12

This *Magic Flute* appetizer never fails to get a laugh. A delicious and classic combination of smoked salmon, tomatoes, and capers becomes a festive conversation starter with an easy trick. All you need is a simple baguette, a sharp knife, a little cream cheese, a few olive slices, and a good sense of humor. Sometimes you just have to play with your food.

1 baguette

8 ounces whipped cream cheese

¼ pound thinly sliced smoked salmon

2 tablespoons capers, drained

Freshly squeezed juice of 1 lemon

1 tomato, thinly sliced

1 small purple onion, thinly sliced

Salt and freshly milled black pepper

Sliced green or black olives, as garnish

Place the bread on a work surface and, using a sharp knife, trim off the ends. Cut the bread in half lengthwise. Remove and discard most of the soft dough in the center to create a hollow. Generously spread whipped cream cheese onto each piece of bread. Lay the salmon and capers onto the bottom section of bread and drizzle with lemon juice. Top with the tomato and onion slices and season to taste with salt and pepper. Close the sandwich.

Decorate the sandwich to look like a flute by placing the sliced olives along the top to look like the holes and keys, using a dab of whipped cream cheese to attach each piece of olive.

Hermann Prey and Nicolai Gedda in *The Magic Flute*

OPERA NOTE

The Met's production of *Die Zauberflöte* designed by Marc Chagall (1966–1967 season; debut February 19, 1967) enchanted audiences with its swirling vibrancy; Speight Jenkins, Jr., of the *Times Herald* reported, "The colors and Chagall's use of them defy description." It was also the occasion for the debut of Lucia Popp as the Queen of the Night.

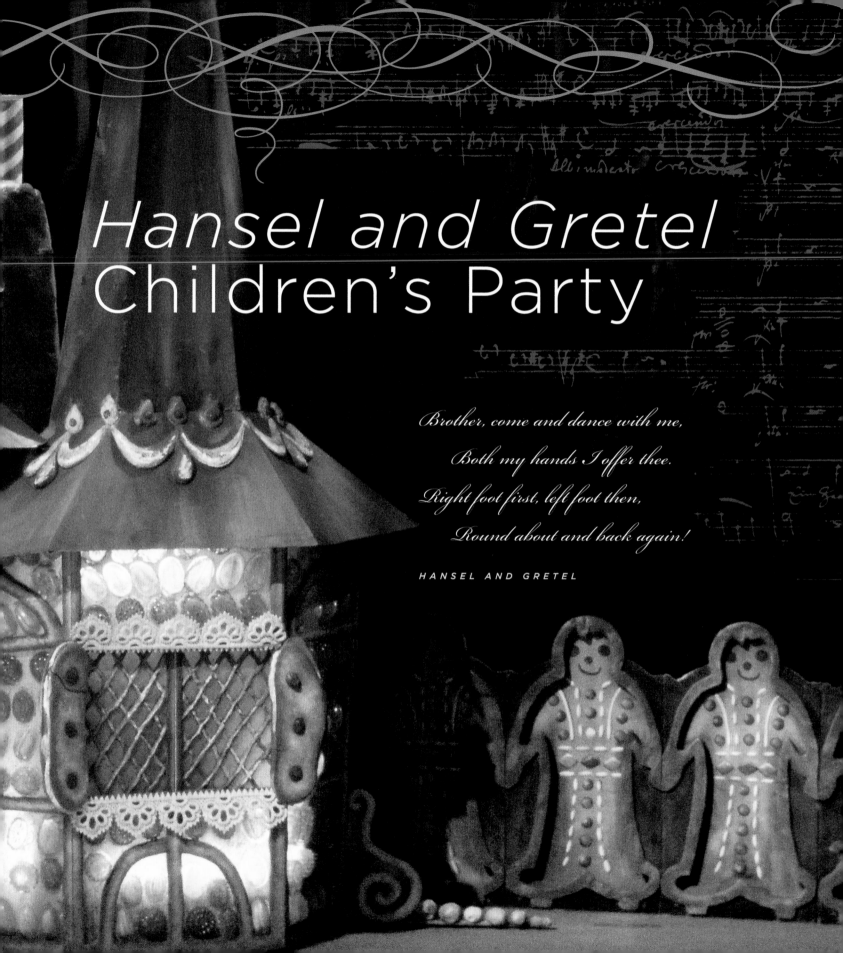

Chapter Twelve

Hansel and Gretel
Children's Party

Brother, come and dance with me,
Both my hands I offer thee.
Right foot first, left foot then,
Round about and back again!

HANSEL AND GRETEL

WHAT BETTER WAY TO INTRODUCE YOUR CHILD TO OPERA'S MAGIC than by hosting a *Hansel and Gretel* party? The operatic version of *Hansel and Gretel*, with a much more child-friendly plot than the Brothers Grimm story, adds charming additional characters like a broom-making father, the Dew Fairy, and angels. It's a perfect first opera filled with wonderful scenes that inspire crafts, foods, and fun party activities.

Imagine the children's squeals of laughter as they go on a scavenger hunt searching for sweets to decorate the witch's house and their delight at creating a miniature candy-studded cookie house while listening to the "Song of the Gingerbread Children." They will love nibbling on the candy house as well as wholesome and fun-to-eat treats like Dew Fairy Pretzel Wands and Gingerbread Man Sandwiches. End this magical party with Angel's Cake and Forest Strawberries Milk Shakes.

Menu

CRAFTS & ACTIVITIES

Decorate a Gingerbread Man

Gather "Strawberries" in the Woods

Make a Dollhouse Broom

Make a Puppet

Dress Up

Make a Flower Wreath

Eat the Witch's House

BEVERAGES

Sandman's Soda

Forest Strawberries Milk Shake

TREATS

Yummy Gingerbread Houses

Dew Fairy Pretzel Wands

Hansel's Raisin and Almond Celery Treats

Gingerbread Man Sandwiches

Angel's Cake

Crafts & Activities

MANY OF MY FONDEST CHILDHOOD MEMORIES center around whimsical parties my mother hosted. She would use almost any excuse to give a party. She made an "I Learned to Tie My Shoe Party," a "First Saturday in Spring Party," and even treated a few of my closest friends and me to a party to celebrate our starting to write in script.

These were small and very simple affairs. There were no gifts, no children's party planners, no clowns, no petting zoo, and no hired entertainers of any sort. The parties never lasted more than an hour, and the guest list included only two or three friends. The thing that made it a party was just, well, calling it a party.

Her style taught me an important parenting lesson. Simple things can still be magical. For a young child, it does not take much to make a party.

You and your child will have more fun if you follow my mother's three S party rules—keep it small, short, and simple.

For children under five, invite no more than two or three guests and for six- to ten-year-olds no more than five guests. Have the party last only one to one and a half hours and aim for only one or two activities.

DECORATE A GINGERBREAD MAN

In the opera, the witch's yard is filled with gingerbread men, which are actually children who are under the witch's enchantment. When Gretel reverses the incantation, all the gingerbread men turn back into children.

Bake, or purchase ready-made from a bakery, large plain gingerbread man cookies. Set out an assortment of decorating icings that the guests can use to draw features or to attach candy features onto the cookies.

GATHER "STRAWBERRIES" IN THE WOODS

Hansel and Gretel are sent into the woods by their mother to gather strawberries. The children can act out that scene by gathering as many small red balloon "strawberries" as they can, while the music from *Hansel and Gretel* plays in the background.

Scatter the balloons around the room and give each child a large brown paper bag or pretty basket to put them in.

OPERA NOTE

Hansel and Gretel, the story of a sister and her brother, was a real-life brother-and-sister collaboration. Engelbert Humperdinck wrote the music, and his sister, Adelheid, wrote the story based on the Brothers' Grimm fairy tale.

Opera Note

In the operatic version of *Hansel and Gretel*,
the children are sent into the woods by
their mother to gather strawberries but
become lost. Over the course of the night,
the Sandman and fourteen angels
help them. In the morning, trying to
find their way home, they stumble upon
the witch's gingerbread house.
She imprisons Hansel and wants to
fatten him up to eat him, but Gretel—
a prototypical feminist superheroine—
saves her brother, kills the witch, and releases
many other children who had been turned
into gingerbread by the witch's spell.

MAKE A DOLLHOUSE BROOM

Hansel and Gretel's father is a broom maker. In their day, brooms were made by hand using branches as handles and straw for the sweeping parts.

Have the guests make doll-sized brooms using simple craft-store finds. Supply each child with a sturdy twig or dowel as the broom's handle. Set out yarn, straw, or hay for the broom's bristles and either wrapped wire, leather craft cord, yarn, or string to tie on the bristles.

Older children may prefer to make full-sized brooms, the supplies for which can be purchased at most craft or hardware stores.

MAKE A PUPPET

Set out craft store supplies so the party guests can make puppets. The puppet's body can be anything from old-fashioned wooden clothespins, to a white sock, or even a paper lunch bag. The children can create any of the characters in the opera: Hansel, Gretel, an angel, the Sandman, the Dew Fairy, a gingerbread child, or the witch.

Provide each child with safety scissors, a glue stick, and an assortment of puppet decorations such as colored pipe cleaners, crayons, markers, sparklers, bits of fabric or felt, and different-colored yarn.

Play snippets of *Hansel and Gretel* in the background while the children create their puppets.

DRESS UP

Hansel and Gretel offers lots of wonderful dress-up opportunities. Set out costume elements in the center of a room, supply full-length mirrors and a little space, and watch the children's imaginations turn wigs, toy brooms, witch's hats, baskets, scarves, boas, and lengths of fabric into Hansel, Gretel, the witch, an angel, and the Dew Fairy.

Play selections from *Hansel and Gretel* while the children dress and act out scenes. Be sure to have a camera ready so you can send photos to each guest's family.

Carol Malone and Paul Franke in *Hansel and Gretel*

MAKE A FLOWER WREATH

In Act II, while Hansel picks strawberries, Gretel makes a garland and wreath of wild roses. As she works she sings, *"There stands a little man in the wood alone, he wears a little mantle of velvet brown . . ."*

Supply the girls with an assortment of small dried or silk flowers, colored ribbons, and glue as well as either a plastic headband or ready-made small grapevine wreath (available in craft stores). The girls can wrap each headband in ribbon and then glue on flowers for a wearable flower wreath of their own, or they can attach the flowers to the grapevine wreath to make a room decoration. If the children are old enough, they can use a glue gun to attach the flowers.

As the girls work, play the aria that Gretel sings when she's making her wreath.

EAT THE WITCH'S HOUSE

Draw a basic picture of a house on a large foam-core board, available at stationery stores. Then, using icing, attach all sorts of candies to the board, decorating it to look like the witch's gingerbread house. Have the children pretend to be Hansel and pick off pieces of the witch's house.

An alternative to drawing the house is to attach the candies, again with thick edible icing, to the outside of a clean dollhouse.

Beverages

SANDMAN'S SODA
Serves 4

Lost in the woods, Hansel and Gretel meet the Sandman, who gently lulls them to sleep with a sprinkling of his special powder.

The children will love sprinkling their own "sandman powder" into this sparkling lemonade.

> **4 cups sparkling water**
> **Freshly squeezed juice of 4 lemons**
> **8 to 12 tablespoons raw or brown sugar**

Fill 4 glasses with ice. Pour 1 cup of sparkling water into each glass and top with the juice of 1 lemon.

Give each child a glass, a stirrer, and a tiny paper cup filled with 2 to 3 tablespoons of sugar "sandman powder."

I shut the children's peepers, shh!

And guard the little sleepers, shh! . . .

Then from the starry sphere above

The angels come with peace and love

And send the children happy dreams

while watch they keep.

HANSEL AND GRETEL

FOREST STRAWBERRIES MILK SHAKE
Serves 4

Hansel and Gretel's mother sends them into the forest to gather wild strawberries. Here, strawberries and bananas make a delicious milk shake.

> **1 pint strawberries**
> **2 cups whole milk**
> **2 bananas, peeled and sliced**
> **1 cup vanilla ice cream or frozen yogurt**

Set 4 strawberries aside to use as garnish. Combine the milk, the remaining strawberries, the bananas, and the ice cream in a blender and puree until smooth. Pour into 4 tall glasses and garnish each with a strawberry.

Treats

ARRANGE A SCAVENGER HUNT. Put the candies that will be used to decorate the gingerbread houses into sturdy zip-top plastic bags. Fill at least twice as many bags as guests so each child has the chance to find more than one. Be sure to explain to the children at the start of the game that *all* the candy found is to be shared.

Hide the bags in accessible places, such as behind the pillows on the couch, on a low bookshelf, or in a simple-to-open chest or cabinet.

If the children can read, write out clues to the hiding places or, if they are too young to read, give verbal clues one at a time. For example, you can hide a bag near the desserts and then tell the children to look near something Hansel likes to eat.

Once all the candy is found, the children pool the goodies for decorating their gingerbread houses.

YUMMY GINGERBREAD HOUSES
Makes 4 houses

We usually associate gingerbread houses with the Christmas holidays, but because the opera *Hansel and Gretel* is set in the summer, this is a chance to decorate one twice a year!

It's as much fun shopping for the candy for the gingerbread houses as it is to watch the children's delight in making them. Select all sorts of colors and shapes so the children have lots of choices for doors, windows, roof shingles, and trim. Pick sweets that can be used to create the environs around the gingerbread house, too. Animal cookies can populate the backyard. Crushed Oreos can become the garden soil, fruit roll-ups can be sculpted into veggies and flowers, and extra upside-down ice cream cones coated in green icing can be trees.

Instead of baking gingerbread, I use ready-made graham crackers, but you can substitute any flat square or rectangular cookie you like. The assembly is easy enough for three-year-olds, thanks to the milk carton "foundation" and easy-to-spread supermarket icing or peanut butter "cement."

4 pint-sized milk or cream cartons, rinsed clean

4 small disposable baking pans

4 jars ready-made vanilla frosting, or peanut butter, for cement

4 small tubes green icing

4 small tubes red icing

Graham crackers

Assorted treats for decorating, such as:

Necco wafers (for shingles or the walkway)

Shredded wheat cereal (for hay or thatch roofing)

Cotton candy (for chimney smoke)

M&Ms, Dots, Life Savers, licorice laces, candy canes, gum drops, round mints, candy pebbles, etc. (for details)

Ice cream cones (for trees)

Fruit leather in various colors (blue for a lake, other colors for flowers and veggies)

Gummy bears, animal crackers (for pets or wildlife)

Green sprinkles, green spearmint jelly leaves (for grass and bushes)

Marshmallows (for sheep)

Thin pretzel sticks (for sheep's legs)

Marzipan (for sculpting)

Assorted colors sparkling sugar

Sweetened coconut mixed with green food coloring

Oreo cookies, crumbled

Food coloring

On a child-friendly surface, set out a work station for each guest including a milk carton, disposable pan, butter knife, jar of frosting, a green and a red tube of icing, paper plate full of graham crackers, and a paper plate full of assorted candies. Keep the coconut "grass" and the Oreo cookie crumb "garden soil" on large platters within reach of everyone.

Help the children as they use the butter knife to coat the bottom of the carton with icing and stick it onto the baking pan. Then they will spread icing on the carton and attach the crackers. Additional dabs of icing can be used to adhere the candy. The small tubes of icing provide color and can be used to create details like doorknobs and trim.

Cookies can also be used to create a walkway or patio in the baking pan. Gummy bears, graham bears, or animal cookies can populate the scene or become the gingerbread children fence, as in the opera.

Sprinkle crushed Oreo cookie crumbs around the house and walkway and plant candy "flowers." Use the green-tinted coconut as "grass." Create fluffy sheep and lambs with a marshmallow, icing, and a little imagination. Create trees by tinting some icing green, spreading it onto ice cream cones, and sprinkling on green coconut or green sparkling sugar. Mix a little blue dye into the icing or use blue fruit leather for a pond, which can be populated with marzipan-sculpted fish. The pond can be circled with those wonderful candies that look like speckled pebbles.

The Children's Chorus in *Hansel and Gretel*

OPERA NOTE

Hansel and Gretel was the first full opera to be on the radio. It was broadcast from Covent Garden, London, in 1923. It was also the first opera broadcast from the Metropolitan Opera House, on Christmas Day, 1931.

Composer Richard Strauss declared *Hansel and Gretel* a masterpiece and conducted the premiere in Weimar on December 23, 1893.

Tradition remains unchanged; it is still often performed at Christmastime.

DEW FAIRY PRETZEL WANDS
Makes 8 wands

The Dew Fairy shakes dewdrops on Hansel and Gretel to wake them after their night in the forest.

To a child's eye, seeing flour and water turn into a delicious treat is like magic. My children, now both older teenagers, still list baking pretzel wands as one of their favorite childhood memories. Take a few minutes, make them with your child, and create your own beautiful memories.

These yummy Dew Fairy pretzel wands, sparkling with pretty multicolored sugar crystals, will light up your child's eyes.

- 1 package active dry yeast, about ¼ ounce
- 1 tablespoon granulated sugar
- 2½ to 3 cups all-purpose flour, plus more as needed
- 2 tablespoons unsalted butter, softened
- 2 teaspoons salt
- Vegetable oil, for the bowl and baking sheet
- 1 large egg, beaten
- Colored sugar crystals or coarse salt

In a large bowl, combine 1 cup warm water with the yeast and granulated sugar and let rest for 10 minutes to activate the yeast.

Add 1 cup of the flour, the butter, and the salt to the yeast mixture and stir to combine. Continue adding the flour, stirring in ½ cup at a time, until the dough is not sticky. Turn the dough out onto a floured surface and knead it, adding a sprinkle more of flour if needed, until the dough is smooth.

Put the dough into a lightly oiled bowl, cover it with a kitchen cloth, and allow to rise for 1 hour.

Preheat the oven to 450°F. Lightly oil a baking sheet.

Divide the dough into 8 sections and give each child 1 or 2 sections. Have children roll each dough section into a 14- to 16-inch-long wand. Don't worry if the wands seem long and thin. They'll puff up in baking.

Put the pretzels on the prepared baking sheet and, using a pastry brush, coat them with the egg. Sprinkle with sugar or salt. Bake for about 12 minutes, until golden. Allow to cool to room temperature.

HANSEL'S RAISIN AND ALMOND CELERY TREATS
Serves 4

The evil witch tried to fatten up Hansel by feeding him raisins and almonds, but no one will get fattened up eating this healthful snack.

You can prepare these wholesome treats, filled with almond butter and cream cheese, for the children ahead of time, if you like. However, I found that my children enjoyed filling the celery themselves.

- 4 stalks celery, peeled
- ¼ cup almond or peanut butter
- 2 tablespoons honey
- 8 ounces (1 package) cream cheese, softened
- Golden raisins, for topping
- Sliced almonds, for topping

Cut each celery stalk in half, or in thirds if they are very long.

In a bowl, blend the almond butter, honey, and cream cheese until well combined. Fill each celery section with a generous helping of the mixture and top with the raisins and sliced almonds.

I'm up with early dawning
And know who loves the morning
So up, ye sleepers, for the bright day
smiles at you!

HANSEL AND GRETEL

GINGERBREAD MAN SANDWICHES
Serves 4

Healthful gingerbread-colored whole-grain breads and gingerbread man–shaped cookie-cutters turn ordinary sandwiches into a magical party food.

FOR BANANA AND NUTELLA SANDWICHES
8 slices of whole-wheat bread
Nutella
1 banana, peeled and thinly sliced

FOR HAM AND CHEESE SANDWICHES
8 slices pumpernickel bread
4 tablespoons (½ stick) unsalted butter, softened
4 to 6 slices smoked ham
4 slices Muenster cheese

FOR HONEY EGG SALAD SANDWICHES
2 hard-boiled eggs, finely minced
1 tablespoon mayonnaise
1 tablespoon honey
Honey mustard
Salt and freshly milled black pepper
8 slices multigrain bread

For Nutella sandwiches, spread the center area of each bread slice with Nutella. Put banana slices onto the center of 4 slices, then top each with another slice of bread.

For ham sandwiches, butter each slice of bread. Place a slice or two of ham and a slice of cheese in the center of 4 slices, then top each with another slice of bread.

For egg salad sandwiches, combine the eggs, mayonnaise, and honey with a dollop of mustard in a small bowl. Season to taste with salt and pepper and mix well. Spread the center area of 4 of the slices of bread with a portion of the egg salad. Top with the other slice of bread.

Press all the sandwiches to close. Using a gingerbread-shaped cookie-cutter, cut out a gingerbread man from the center section of each sandwich. Arrange the sandwiches on a serving platter.

ANGEL'S CAKE
Serves 8

The fourteen angels who protect the sleeping Hansel and Gretel were the inspiration for this golden, light-as-air angel food cake sweetened with maple syrup. To make it even more dreamy, fill the center with magical-looking fluffy cotton candy, colorful lollipops, or spun sugar.

Unsalted butter, for the pan
10 egg whites
½ teaspoon salt
1 teaspoon cream of tartar
1 cup cake flour, plus more for the pan
1 cup pure maple syrup
1 teaspoon vanilla extract

Preheat the oven to 350°F. Generously butter and flour a Bundt or tube pan. Reserve.

In a large mixing bowl, using an electric mixer set on high, whip the egg whites, salt, and cream of tartar until the egg whites form soft peaks, about 5 minutes. Reduce the mixer speed to medium and slowly add the cake flour and maple syrup until just combined. Blend in the vanilla.

Pour the batter into the prepared Bundt pan and bake until golden, about 35 minutes.

Carefully invert the pan onto a wire rack and allow it to cool upside down, which prevents the cake from falling. Run a knife around the edges to remove the cake.

Product Sources

CHAPTER ONE

For aromatic syrups:

Da Vinci Gourmet
www.davincigourmet.com

GermanDeli.com
www.germandeli.com

Kalustyan's
www.kalustyans.com
123 Lexington Avenue
New York, NY 10016
212-685-3451

Monin Gourmet Flavorings
www.monin.com

For spices and hard-to-find products:

Adriana's Caravan
www.adrianascaravan.com

Coastal Goods
www.coastalgoods.com

Gourmet Country
www.gourmetcountry.com

Ingredients Gourmet Boutique
www.ingredientsgourmet.com

Kalustyan's
www.kalustyans.com
123 Lexington Avenue
New York, NY 10016
212-685-3451

Penzeys Spices
www.penzeys.com

Spice Appeal
www.spice-appeal.com

The Spice House
www.thespicehouse.com

World Merchants
www.worldspice.com

Zingerman's
www.zingermans.com

For vincotto and other quality vinegars:

igourmet.com
www.igourmet.com

For dried guava slices:

Economy Candy
www.economycandy.com
108 Rivington Street
New York, NY 10002
800-352-4544

Oh! Nuts
www.ohnuts.com

For chilie pepper marmalades:

Earth & Vine Provisions
www.earthnvine.com

Hösgood's
www.4garlic.com/santafe.html

Santa Fe School of Cooking
www.santafeschoolofcooking.com

CHAPTER TWO

For spices and Spanish specialty foods:

Casa Oliver
www.casaoliver.com

LaTienda.com
www.tienda.com

The Spanish Table
www.spanishtable.com

For ready-made chocolate "chorizos" or "salami":

Marky's Caviar
www.markyscaviar.com

CHAPTER FOUR

For German and European beers:

Beers of Europe
www.beersofeurope.com

For quality German sausages and cold cuts:

Schaller & Weber
www.schallerweber.com
1654 Second Avenue
New York, NY 10028
212-879-3047

CHAPTER SEVEN

For HP Sauce:

English Tea Store
www.englishteastore.com/hpsauce255g.html

CHAPTER TEN

For information on various vodkas:

Absolut
www.Absolut.com

Skyy Vodka
www.skyyvodka.com

Stolichnaya
www.stoli.com

Smirnoff
www.smirnoff.com

Grey Goose
www.greygoosevodka.com

For fine Russian foods:

Pierogi.com
www.pierogi.com

RussianFoods.com
www.russianfoods.com

For domestic caviar:

Seattle Caviar Company
www.caviar.com
2922 Eastlake Avenue East
Seattle, WA 98102
206-323-3005

For samovars:

Russian Legacy.com
www.russianlegacy.com

The Russian Shop
www.therussianshop.com

Special Teas
www.specialteas.com

Sur La Table
www.surlatable.com

For prepared and packaged Russian specialty items:

M&I International Foods
249 Brighton Beach Avenue
Brighton Beach, NY 11235
718-615-1011

CHAPTER ELEVEN

For preserved Seville oranges:

Cardullo's Gourmet Shoppe
www.cardullos.com/Preserves.htm
6 Brattle Street
Harvard Square
Cambridge, MA 02138
617-491-8888

Credits

WHENEVER POSSIBLE FOR TRANSLATIONS THAT COME FROM LINER NOTES, the date corresponds to the copyright on the translation rather than the recording. If there is no date on the translation, the recording's latest copyright date is given.

CITATIONS

CHAPTER ONE

"Bella vita!" (20)
Angelo Anelli. *L'Italiana in Algeri* (Rossini).
G. Schirmer's Collection of Opera Librettos.
Trans. Ruth and Thomas Martin. Milwaukee, WI:
G. Schirmer, Inc., 1966.

Angelo Anelli. *L'Italiana in Algeri* (Rossini).
Trans. Lionel Salter. Cond. Jesús López Cobos.
Orchestre de Chambre de Lausanne. With Jennifer
Larmore. Teldec, 1989.

"Sarò zeppo e contornato" (31)
Jacopo Ferretti. *La Cenerentola* (Rossini). Trans. Gwyn
Morris. Cond. Riccardo Chailly. Orchestra e coro del
Teatro Comunale di Bologna. With Cecilia Bartoli.
London, 1972.

CHAPTER TWO

"Versa il vino" (35)
Lorenzo da Ponte. *Don Giovanni* (Mozart). Trans. Avril
Bardoni. Cond. Sir Georg Solti. London Philharmonic.
With Bryn Terfel, Renée Fleming. Decca, 1990.

All quotes from *Carmen* (36, 37, 48)
Henri Meilhac and Ludovic Halévy, after Mérimée.
Carmen (Bizet). Trans. Diana Reed. Cond. Georg Solti.
With Tatiana Troyanos, Plácido Domingo. Decca, 1976.

CHAPTER THREE

"L'heure s'envole" (58)
Jules Barbier & Michel Carré. *Roméo et Juliette* (Gounod).
Trans. Joseph Allen. Cond. Alain Lombard. Orchestre et
Chœrs dy Théâtre National de l'Opéra de Paris. With
Franco Corelli, Mirella Freni. EMI Classics, 1969.

"Vin ou bière" (59)
Jules Barbier and Michel Carré, after Goethe. *Faust*
(Gounod). Trans. Peggie Cochrane. Cond. Richard
Bonynge. With Joan Sutherland, Franco Corelli. Decca, 1991.

"J'aurai grand soin" (62)
Henri Cain. *Don Quichotte* (Massenet). G. Schirmer's
Collection of Opera-Librettos. New York: G. Schirmer, 1911.

CHAPTER FOUR

"Nur wer der Minne Macht entsagt" (75) &
"Von Freias Frucht" (90)
Richard Wagner. *Das Rheingold*. Cond. Sir Georg Solti.
Wiener Philharmoniker. With George London, Kirsten
Flagstad. Decca.

"Ein Souper heut uns winkt" (78), "Ich lade gern mir
Gäste ein" (82), & "Die Majestät wird anerkannt" (86)
Carl Haffner & Richard Genée. *Die Fledermaus*
(J. Strauss, Jr.). Trans. Robert A. Jordan. Cond. André
Previn. Wiener Philharmoniker. With Kiri Te Kanawa.
Philips, 1991.

Opera Note (81). Taken from "Ringmaster," Dr. Elise K.
Kirk. *Opera News,* March 27, 1993. Copyright © 1993
The Metropolitan Opera Guild, Inc.

CHAPTER SIX

"Tutto nel mondo" (107)
Arrigo Boito. *Falstaff* (Verdi). Trans. Mary Jane Phillips-
Matz. New York: Metropolitan Opera Guild, Inc., 1992.

"Libiamo" (113)
Francesco Maria Piave. *La Traviata* (Verdi). Trans. David
Stivender. New York: Metropolitan Opera Guild, Inc., 1989.

CHAPTER EIGHT

"Viva il vino spumeggiante" (139)
Giovanni Targioni-Tozzetti and Guido Menasci. *Cavalleria Rusticana* (Mascagni). Cond. Gabriele Santini. Orchestrae Coro del Teatro dell'Opera di Roma. With Victoria de los Angeles, Franco Corelli. EMI Classics, 1991.

CHAPTER TEN

"In joy and merriment…" (167)
Modest Tchaikovsky after Pushkin. *Pique Dame* (Tchaikovsky). Trans. Martin Cooper. Cond. Valery Gergiev. With Gegam Grigorian. Philips, 1993.

Quotes from *Love for Three Oranges* (169, 175)
Sergei Prokofiev. *Love for Three Oranges* (Prokofiev). Translation and transliteration by Andrew Huth. Cond. Valery Gergiev. With Evgeny Akimov. Philips, 2000.

Quotes from *War and Peace* (171, 178, 180)
Sergei Prokofiev and Mira Mendelson. *War and Peace* (Prokofiev). Translation by Jane Iles and transliteration by Helena Bayliss. Cond. Richard Hickox. Spoleto Festival Orchestra. With Ekaterina Morozova, Roderick Williams. Chandos, 1992.

CHAPTER ELEVEN

"Tocca e bevi!" (187)
Lorenzo da Ponte. *Così Fan tutte* (Mozart). Trans. Lindsay Craig. Cond. Jean-Claude Malgoire. La Grande Écurie and la Chambre du Roy. With Sophie Fournier, Laura Polverelli. Naïve, 2005.

"Finch'han dal vino" (190)
Lorenzo da Ponte. *Don Giovanni* (Mozart). Trans. Lindsay Craig. Cond. Jean-Claude Malgoire. La Grande Écurie and la Chambre du Roy. With Nicolas Rivenq, Danielle Borst. Naïve, 2005.

"Ma signor" (193)
Lorenzo da Ponte. *Le Nozze di Figaro* (Mozart). Trans. Lionel Salter, with kind permission of Warner Classics. With Danielle Borst, Hubert Claessens. Naïve, 2005.

CHAPTER TWELVE

Quotes from *Hansel and Gretel* (197, 202, 207)
Adelheid Wette. *Hänsel und Gretel* (Humperdinck). New York: Fred. Rullman, Inc., 1925.

PHOTOGRAPH CREDITS

Photograph © 2006 Beth Bergman: 2, 32–33, 53, 66, 68, 94–95, 105, 166–67, 171, 174, 176, 182–83, 224, jacket back

Andrew Eccles, courtesy of Decca: 71

William Harris, courtesy of *Opera News*: 5, 6, 9, 12–13, 18, 43, 83, 86, 99, 119, 150–51, 161, 163, 165, 189, 216

Robert Kusel, courtesy of Lyric Opera of Chicago: 125, 135

Courtesy of *Opera News*: 20, 25, 37, 49, 58, 63, 74–75, 88, 93, 106–7, 114, 138–39, 149, 153

Carol Rosegg, courtesy of New York City Opera: 120–21

© 2006 Beatriz Schiller: 54–55

Wist Thorpe, courtesy of *Opera News*: 196–97, 201, 205

Conversions

VOLUME EQUIVALENTS

These are not exact equivalents for American cups and spoons, but have been rounded up or down slightly to make measuring easier.

AMERICAN	METRIC	IMPERIAL
¼ t	1.2 ml	
½ t	2.5 ml	
1 t	5.0 ml	
½ T (1.5 t)	7.5 ml	
1 T (3 t)	15 ml	
¼ cup (4 T)	60 ml	2 fl oz
⅓ cup (5 T)	75 ml	2½ fl oz
½ cup (8 T)	125 ml	4 fl oz
⅔ cup (10 T)	150 ml	5 fl oz
¾ cup (12 T)	175 ml	6 fl oz
1 cup (16 T)	250 ml	8 fl oz
1¼ cups	300 ml	10 fl oz (½ pt)
1½ cups	350 ml	12 fl oz
2 cups (1 pint)	500 ml	16 fl oz
2½ cups	625 ml	20 fl oz (1 pt)
1 quart	1 l	32 fl oz

OVEN TEMPERATURE EQUIVALENTS

OVEN MARK	F	C	GAS
Very cool	250–275	130–140	½–1
Cool	300	150	2
Warm	325	170	3
Moderate	350	180	4
Moderately hot	375	190	5
	400	200	6
Hot	425	220	7
	450	230	8
Very hot	475	250	9

WEIGHT EQUIVALENTS

The metric weights given in this chart are not exact equivalents, but have been rounded up or down slightly to make measuring easier.

AVOIRDUPOIS	METRIC
¼ oz	7 g
½ oz	15 g
1 oz	30 g
2 oz	60 g
3 oz	90 g
4 oz	115 g
5 oz	150 g
6 oz	175 g
7 oz	200 g
8 oz (½ lb)	225 g
9 oz	250 g
10 oz	300 g
11 oz	325 g
12 oz	350 g
13 oz	375 g
14 oz	400 g
15 oz	425 g
16 oz (1 lb)	450 g
1½ lb	750 g
2 lb	900 g
2¼ lb	1 kg
3 lb	1.4 kg
4 lb	1.8 kg

INDEX

Page numbers in *italic* refer to illustrations.

A

Aida, 119, *119*
Ale. *See* Beer and ale
Almond(s):
  cake accented with citrus, 52
  chocolate macaroons, 71
  harem honey custard, 194
  Isolde's marzipan kisses, 93
  linguine *Il Trittico* with oranges, apricots and, *158, 159*
  linzertorte music bars, *186,* 187
  and raisin celery treats, Hansel's, 207
Amaretti roasted peaches, Nedda's, 149
Amaretto-rum balls, 119
American artisanal cheeses with mint julep jam and bloody mary marmalade, 99
Andalusia (cocktail), 37
Angel's cake, 208, *209*
Appetizers and hors d'oeuvres:
  black lacquer teriyaki wings, 156, *157*
  charcuterie platter with three homemade mustards, *79,* 80–81
  French canapés, 64, *65*
  herbes de Provence onion tart, 68
  Magic Flute savory surprise, 195
  Mamma Lucia's sweet and tangy eggplant caponata, 141
  pâté Manon with Chambord glaze, 67
  Ping, Pang, and Pong pork nibbles, 156
  tapenade red potato bites, 69
  tournedos Rossini, 21
  Les Troyens smoked trout custard, 69

Turandot tea eggs, 154, *155*
  warm cheese puffs, 66
  see also Cheese platters; Salads; Soups; Tapas; *Zakuski*
Apple(s):
  and butternut squash "hash" with Southern Comfort, *100,* 101
  crisps (garnish), *126,* 127
  golden, with kale, Freia's, 90, *91*
  harvest cocktail, sparkling, 97
  martini, *William Tell,* 15
  tasting, 97
  William Tell Act III (cocktail), 15
Apricot(s):
  linguine *Il Trittico* with oranges, almonds and, *158,* 159
  miniature sachertorte, 185
  poppy seed cake, flourless, 92
Ariadne auf Naxos, 76, 89
Artichokes, Roman-style crispy, 163
Asparagus, white, with strawberry champagne vinaigrette, 86
Assigning seats at dinner parties, 17

B

Bagna cauda, 146
Banana and Nutella sandwiches, 208
Barbiere di Siviglia, Il, 43
Beef:
  filet mignon, in tournedos Rossini, 21
  Mrs. Lovett's meat pies, 128
  roll, Sicilian stuffed, 144
  Scotch eggs, 128, *129*
  shepherd's pie, 132
Beer and ale:
  beer flip, 125
  German, 77
  shandy, 123
  tasting of, 123
Beethoven, Ludwig van, 92, 110
Beets, in golden borscht shots, 176
Bel canto dinner party, 12–31

Bellini:
  classic, 15
  martini, 16
Bellini, Vincenzo, 14, 24
Bel Paese, 17
  with hot pepper marmalade, 19
Benvenuto Cellini, 56
Berlioz, Hector, 56, 69
Beverages, alcoholic:
  cream di limoncella, 31
  English bishop, 124
  tarantara hot toddy, 124
  see also Beer and ale; Cocktails; Wine
Beverages, nonalcoholic:
  forest strawberries milk shake, 202
  hot chocolate, 189
  Sandman's soda, 202
Biscuits, maple buttermilk, melt-in-your-mouth, *100,* 101
Bizet, Georges, 37, 49, 64
  tapas party with *Carmen,* 32–53
Black lacquer teriyaki wings, 156, *157*
Black Russian (cocktail), 171
Blini:
  buckwheat, caviar with, *172,* 173
  sweet potato, mushroom "caviar" with, 177
Bloody mary marmalade, 99
Bohème, La, 150–51, 163, *163,* 164, *165*
La Bohème fruit and nut fantasy, 165
Borscht shots, golden, 176
Breads:
  focaccia con rosmarino, 114
  Little Buttercup scones with assorted preserves, 136
  Russian sweet, with orange icing, 179
Broccoli rabe, sautéed, with red pepper garlic crisps, 28
Brooms, doll-sized, 200
Brunch dishes:
  apple and butternut squash "hash" with Southern Comfort, *100,* 101

La commedia è finita!

PAGLIACCI

PAGE 216: *L' Italiana in Algeri*